Finally a book about the Rorschach for use in everyday clinical practice. *Assessment Using the Rorschach Inkblot Test* presents a welcome antidote to generations of cumbersome scoring systems. Written in an accessible style, it provides cogent instruction on administration, person-centered interpretation, and communicating findings in test reports.

—**Lon Gieser, PhD,** Independent Practice, Upper Montclair, NJ, and Editor, *Evocative Images: The Thematic Apperception Test and the Art of Projection*

Choca and Rossini have developed a timely and time efficient Rorschach technique that is clear, concise, and accessible.

—**Gary Groth-Marnat, PhD, ABPP, ABAP,** Pacifica Graduate Institute, Santa Barbara, CA

In casual, lighthearted, and easy-to-read prose, Choca and Rossini rely on their years of clinical acumen with the Rorschach to propose modifications of the two dominant systems in use today to help clinicians simplify administration, coding, and interpretation and find "the person behind the scores."

—**Gregory J. Meyer, PhD,** Professor, Department of Psychology, University of Toledo, Toledo, OH

This is an important book for all assessment psychologists. The most critical feature is that it will make any professional reader think carefully about the Rorschach. It is a major step in Rorschach research.

—**Barry Ritzler, PhD,** Professor Emeritus, Long Island University, Brooklyn, NY, and Past President of the Society for Personality Assessment

Good things come in small packages. This is a fecund, low *Lambda* gem: brief but richly variegated, economical yet erudite, utterly saturated with blended wisdom. Unafraid of rocking the boat, necessarily wrestling with Cronbach's Ghost (achieving a partial takedown), Choca and Rossini present an alternate, abbreviated four-card procedure (nicknamed "Herm," of course). This is a go-to guide for anyone who wishes to give the Rorschach a 21st-century makeover. Choca and Rossini will enliven your *Erlebnistyp*!

—**Charles A. Peterson, PhD, ABAP, LP,** Independent Practice, St. Paul, MN

Assessment Using the Rorschach Inkblot Test

Psychological Assessment Series

Assessment Using the MMPI–2–RF
David M. McCord

Assessment Using the Rorschach Inkblot Test
James P. Choca and Edward D. Rossini

Psychological Assessment Series

Assessment Using the Rorschach Inkblot Test

James P. Choca
Edward D. Rossini

AMERICAN PSYCHOLOGICAL ASSOCIATION
Washington, DC

Published by
American Psychological Association
750 First Street, NE
Washington, DC 20002
www.apa.org

APA Order Department
P.O. Box 92984
Washington, DC 20090-2984
Phone: (800) 374-2721; Direct: (202) 336-5510
Fax: (202) 336-5502; TDD/TTY: (202) 336-6123
Online: http://www.apa.org/pubs/books
E-mail: order@apa.org

In the U.K., Europe, Africa, and the Middle East, copies may be ordered from
Eurospan Group
c/o Turpin Distribution
Pegasus Drive
Biggleswade Bedfordshire
SG18 8TQ United Kingdom
Phone: +44 (0) 1767 604972
Fax: +44 (0) 1767 601640
Online: https://www.eurospanbookstore.com/apa
E-mail: eurospan@turpin-distribution.com

Typeset in Meridien by Circle Graphics, Inc., Columbia, MD

Printer: Sheridan Books, Chelsea, MI
Cover Designer: Mercury Publishing Services, Inc., Rockville, MD

Library of Congress Cataloging-in-Publication Data

Names: Choca, James, 1945- author. | Rossini, Edward, author.
Title: Assessment using the Rorschach Inkblot Test / James P. Choca and
    Edward D. Rossini.
Description: Washington, DC : American Psychological Association, [2018] |
Series: Psychological assessment series | Includes bibliographical
    references and index.
Identifiers: LCCN 2017038839 | ISBN 9781433828812 | ISBN 1433828812
Subjects: LCSH: Rorschach Test.
Classification: LCC BF698.8.R5 C458 2018 | DDC 155.2/842—dc23 LC record available at
https://lccn.loc.gov/2017038839

British Library Cataloguing-in-Publication Data
A CIP record is available from the British Library.

Printed in the United States of America
First Edition

http://dx.doi.org/10.1037/0000075-000

10 9 8 7 6 5 4 3 2 1

To our wives, Monica Choca and Janice Kowalski, for helping us with the texture and color of our own Rorschach protocols, and for an amount of encouragement and support that the Rorschach inkblots cannot measure.

Contents

About the Series

To conduct a thorough and informative psychological assessment, practitioners need to master a complex set of skills that go beyond the rote procedures laid out in a test manual. The Psychological Assessment Series features brief, practical books by veteran practitioners who synthesize their professional wisdom into expert tips and insights for conducting a wide range of educational and psychological assessments. Each book provides context for using a specific test, including the history of its development and its current uses, followed by recommendations on when to use the test and how to combine it with other assessment tools, step-by-step instructions for administration, advice for navigating challenging scenarios, and guidance on how to use or adapt the test for a particular population of clients or, for example, when diagnosing a specific disorder, evaluating personality traits, and monitoring treatment or other interventions. All volumes in this series can be used as both educational tools for graduate students in assessment courses and handy references for practitioners. Each book can be paired with a companion video that features the author demonstrating the assessment process in real time, followed by an analysis that highlights significant moments from the demonstration along with key takeaways for practice. The books and videos may be used independently, but together they make an ideal learning tool for students and trainees.

Acknowledgments

(JPC) am thankful for the discussions and collaborations with Chilean Professor Hellmut Brinkmann. We would like to thank our APA Books contacts and editors, including Linda Malnasi McCarter, David Becker, Hyde Loomis, and Elizabeth V. Brace.

I (EDR) would like to thank Dr. James P. Choca, Dr. Karen L. Eggen, Dr. Janice M. Kowalski, Dr. Jeri Morris, Dr. John M. Paolella, Dr. Therese M. Unumb, and the late Dr. James C. Young. Masterful clinical psychologists and wordsmiths all, talking with them about assessment clients and studying their reports has taught me more than I ever thanked them for.

Assessment Using the Rorschach Inkblot Test

Introduction

T he Rorschach Test (Rorschach, 1921/1942) is the most famous psychological test ever invented. It is also the most controversial. To become
a Rorschacher, you need to resolve that cognitive dissonance. Our
intent is to deal with the Rorschach's ongoing identity crisis. Once
you have an understanding of what the Rorschach really is, adapting it for
your specific assessment needs is a sensible next step. We will walk you
through that process.

Our goal is to simplify the administration, scoring, and interpretation of
the Rorschach by making the process less cumbersome, briefer, more practical, and more person centered. We begin by addressing the most nagging
Rorschach question—What is it, really?—and by offering our remedy to its
identity crisis (Chapter 1). In subsequent chapters, we guide you through
our model of administration (Chapter 2) and our proposed method for scoring and interpreting the variables with our short-form and simplified coding

Supporting materials for this book can be downloaded from the following companion website:
http://pubs.apa.org/books/supp/choca. These materials include three appendixes that summarize and compare the results of two meta-analyses, one of published Comprehensive System
community norms (Muñoz, Choca, Rossini, & Garside, 2011) and the other of unpublished
psychiatric norms. The companion site also features full sample case reports similar to the one
presented in Exhibit 8.1. Proper steps were taken to protect the confidentiality of all individuals
mentioned in these case reports.

http://dx.doi.org/10.1037/0000075-001
Assessment Using the Rorschach Inkblot Test, by J. P. Choca and E. D. Rossini

system that we call the Basic Rorschach (BR; Chapters 3–6).[1] Although the BR is the primary focus of these chapters, we also review the two main Rorschach scoring systems: the Comprehensive System (CS; Exner, 2003) and the Rorschach Performance Assessment System (R-PAS; Meyer, Viglione, Mihura, Erard, & Erdberg, 2011).

We first introduce scoring by reviewing the 10 broad areas that all Rorschach scoring systems focus on (Chapter 3). Then, we provide a detailed review of the individual variables that make up the Structural Summary (Chapter 4), including how to consider these variables alongside one another (Chapter 5). After reviewing the mechanics of scoring these variables, we provide a step-by-step framework as well as advanced interpretation strategies that can be used to find a deeper meaning behind these scores (Chapter 6).

We then make our plea for keeping the client in mind (Chapter 7), present report-writing guidelines (Chapter 8), and propose a shorter test called "Herm" that uses four cards instead of the standard 10, as well as expressing our hopes for the future of the Rorschach (Chapter 9). Throughout this book, we focus on older adolescent and adult assessment; specialized textbooks for assessing school-age children are available.

The Rorschach is neither an omniscient nor an infallible test, and early assessors oversold its value. At its peak, the Rorschach was estimated to have been administered a million times a year. Yet, throughout its history, the Rorschach has been a shape-shifter, adapting to whatever psychological theories were in fashion. It is certainly a venerable, multicultural, lifespan, and pantheoretical test. Unfortunately, both academic disputes and economic forces have converged in reducing its presence in doctoral training and its use in assessment practice (C. Piotrowski, 2015a, 2015b).

However, within assessment psychology, excitement reigns for all things Rorschach. There is an intense intellectual and commercial competition between the established Rorschach coding and interpretive systems, the CS (Exner, 2003) and the newer R-PAS (Meyer, Viglione, Mihura, Erard, & Erdberg, 2011). This competition has generated a sophisticated body of empirical research, some of it more complex than is useful for the casual reader. For frontline assessors, both camps have also published detailed case studies as teaching tools.

There may not be a better time to become a Rorschach assessor: The field has opened up for new ideas with the passing of John Exner, who developed the CS and published it in 1974. However, Rorschach use is decreasing, and some have predicted its ultimate extinction (Paul, 2004). We hope to help save it from that fate with proposals that restrict its use to its areas of excellence and simplify its methodology.

The primary audiences for this book are graduate students taking their initial personality assessment courses, practicum and internship students in clinical and counseling psychology, and their instructors and supervisors. Other audiences include early or mid-

---

[1]A computer program, called "Hermann," for entering, scoring, and computing the calculations of a Rorschach protocol can be found at http://www.choca-assessments.com.

level clinical psychologists seeking to retool their skill set in projective assessment using the Rorschach and seasoned practitioners who feel constrained by the CS and R-PAS systems. Finally, several novel ideas of ours will be introduced in this book for beginner and veteran Rorschachers alike, including our simplified coding system (the BR) and a shortened, four-card Rorschach test (Herm).

Our recommendation to graduate students is to read this book chapter by chapter like any other textbook. More experienced assessors will likely jump to the interpretation chapters to see what any specific atypical score (marker) can mean. Either way, as textbook or pick-and-choose reference text, we welcome you to the Rorschach world.

Overview of the Rorschach

Identity Crisis

1

Yesterday, upon the stair
I met a man who wasn't there
He wasn't there again today
I wish, I wish he'd go away . . .
—*William Hughes Mearns*

The metaphoric man on the staircase in William Hughes Mearns's (1899/ 2000) poem about a haunted house, *Antigonish*, could be Hermann Rorschach's test: delightfully alive to some of us, but powerfully wished away forever by others, mainly American research psychologists. These extreme opinions have been expressed in the psychological community since Rorschach's German monograph was translated into English in 1942 (Rorschach, 1921/1942). There is no chance that either side will convince the other.

The goal of this chapter is to introduce you to the Rorschach identity crisis. Most people have heard of the inkblot test, and many people have seen some of the inkblots in an introductory course textbook or online. As Kleiger (2015) noted, "Over the last century, Hermann Rorschach's creative experiment has imbedded itself in our society and captured the imagination of generations of clinicians, researchers, artists, writers, and the lay public in general" (p. 221).

http://dx.doi.org/10.1037/0000075-002
Assessment Using the Rorschach Inkblot Test, by J. P. Choca and E. D. Rossini

What Is the Rorschach?

Let's begin with the basics. The Rorschach is a visual problem-solving task that has not changed in nearly 100 years. People are instructed to answer one and only one question, the same question, for each of the 10 cards presented in a fixed order and in a fixed spatial position: "What might this be?" The administration involves several phases that are described in the next chapter. Clinicians essentially ask themselves, "How come?" for each response (i.e., which elements of visual perception were used for each response). Everything the client says is recorded verbatim, including asides, swear words, and expressions of emotional reaction.

The actual inkblots have not changed since 1921. They are produced by only one publisher, Verlag Hans Huber, in Bern, Switzerland. The cards have a standard size and are reproduced on rectangular, hard-backed, somewhat shiny, rigid white card stock that can endure lots of handling. The actual inkblots are fairly, but not perfectly, symmetrical. The cards are identified by Roman numerals. Five of the cards (I, IV, V, VI, and VII) are entirely achromatic (black and white), and five include chromatic colors, either partially (II, III) or totally (VIII, IX, X). Most examiners use commercially published miniature (one-page) charts to document Location and formatted sheets to write down all responses. Adept keyboarders now use laptops or tablets to record responses, and the senior author (JCP) offers Hermann, an unlimited-use program for Rorschach transcription and data summary (Choca, 2017).[1]

Recent discussions about the effect of viewing the Rorschach cards online conclude that casually seeing the cards does not pose a serious challenge for real-life assessment (e.g., Schultz & Loving, 2012). However, in a perfect world, the actual plates would have been protected from online viewing.

Once the Rorschach basics are understood, beginners need to confront several conceptual issues. First, they need to understand what the Rorschach is (and is not). Unfortunately, the Rorschach has an identity problem. What is it, really? Whether seen as a psychometric test, a clinical instrument, a semistructured interview, a personality inventory, a projective technique, a performance-based measure, or simply an assessment method, its basic identity remains hard to pin down. How you define the Rorschach often dictates how you can use it and how confidently you can present inferences from a person's responses.

The Rorschach's Origins and Evolution

Some additional historical context may help resolve the identity problem. The Rorschach was developed in Europe nearly 100 years ago on adult neuropsychiatric patients. The Rorschach came of age in the United States as an adult test because of

---

[1]The Hermann program can be downloaded from http://www.choca-assessments.com.

the number of psychologists serving as diagnosticians in the military and Veterans Administration medical centers immediately after the Second World War. Psychological testing defined clinical psychology in that era, and those assessors adopted the Rorschach as an exciting addition to the standard test battery.

Its use in the evaluation of civilian patients was initially due to its avid acceptance by the psychoanalytic communities in Chicago and New York City and at the Menninger Clinic in Houston, Texas. The Rorschach remains a frontline assessment tool but is largely removed from its psychoanalytic roots. Yet, in popular culture, the Rorschach continues to have a psychoanalytic aura as an X-ray of the personality, capable of revealing hidden conflicts. Or, as a Turkish Rorschach pioneer stated, "the Rorschach is the radiography of the human spirit" (İkiz, 2011). Hermann Rorschach's biographer (Searls, 2017) noted that Rorschach himself made no such claim. The fusing of the Rorschach with psychoanalytic theory was largely an American phenomenon, due to the influence of David Rapaport at the Menninger Clinic and later codified in Roy Schafer's (1954) book, *Psychoanalytic Interpretation in Rorschach Testing*.

If it is not a psychoanalytic tool, what do Rorschach responses show? An analogy between psychological testing and the components of a song may be useful. The information elicited from a person through an interview or through the Big Three personality inventories, the Minnesota Multiphasic Personality Inventory—2 (Butcher, Dahlstrom, Graham, Tellegen, & Kaemmer, 1989), the Millon Clinical Multiaxial Inventory (Millon, 2016), and the Personality Assessment Inventory (Morey, 1991), resembles a song's lyrics. In contrast, the examinee's observed behavior bears an analogy to the song's underlying melody. The Rorschach is well suited to bring the melody into sharper focus.

Our resolution of its identity crisis is to see the Rorschach as a unique observational method, akin to a psychological magnifying glass. It is a way to (a) observe the operations of a person's unique psychological inclinations—an individual-in-action—across challenging situations and to (b) elicit many underlying forms of psychopathology (e.g., formal thought disorder, affective dyscontrol) or less-than-conscious maladaptive preoccupations, often involving aggression or sexual conflicts. Our resolution of the identity problem is consistent with Weiner's (1994) argument for renaming it the Rorschach Inkblot Method instead of the Rorschach Test. We have no objection to either label. In fact, nearly everybody just refers to it as *the Rorschach*.

The Rorschach Scoring Systems

The Rorschach's popularity was facilitated by the invention of scoring systems that quantified all aspects of an examinee's visual–perceptual experience and verbal responses. These systems make the test look more psychometric and "scientific." For many years, the major coding systems were those of Bruno Klopfer (Klopfer, Ainsworth, Klopfer, & Holt, 1954) and Samuel Beck (1950), rivals who hated each other. The history of the Rorschach is defined by rivalries: psychoanalytic versus perceptual, content interpretation versus structural interpretation, Beck versus Klopfer. The Beck–Klopfer rivalry is now largely forgotten, though we would like to revive some of Klopfer's orientation in Chapter 7.

Another rivalry has emerged. The two major coding and interpretation systems for the Rorschach in the United States are the Comprehensive System (CS; Exner, 2003) and the Rorschach Performance Assessment System (R-PAS; Meyer, Viglione, Mihura, Erard, & Erdberg, 2011). Both systems are thorough, complex, and cumbersome to learn and use regularly without a zealot's passion. Each system has merit, and you should feel free to join either camp as each provides a highly structured Rorschach home. The CS, which was developed by psychologist John Exner, has been used since 1974, and until very recently, most Rorschach research used CS variables. Exner's contribution in developing a consensus scoring system cannot be overstated. It truly provided a common language for practitioners and researchers. However, the coding challenges and interpretive nightmare expanded as the CS evolved with each successive edition of Exner's book. Exner's (1974) relatively brief and simple textbook grew to a less readable, larger tome (Exner, 2003).

The R-PAS was born in 2011 in response to nagging problems with the CS. The prolific researchers of the R-PAS have dominated journal pages for many years. However, most clinicians do not read scientific journals, and the R-PAS remains unknown to many frontline assessment psychologists. Approximately one third of doctoral programs that teach the Rorschach teach the R-PAS, in contrast to the dominance of the CS in training programs (Mihura, Roy, & Graceffo, 2017).

Research on Rorschach Use and Validity

The Rorschach is an "old" test, nearly a centenarian, in continuous use since 1921. Still, the most recent survey of psychological test use indicated that the Rorschach was the eighth most widely used test (Wright et al., 2017). Additionally, the Rorschach has generated a massive research base, a large library of teaching and learning textbooks, and several continuing education centers, and it even has a research center and museum at the University of Bern. The well-recognized *Journal of Personality Assessment* began as Klopfer's informal *Rorschach Research Exchange* in 1936.

The Rorschach is a multiculturally valid assessment technique, with administrative guidelines and interpretive models tailored to specific populations (e.g., Campo, 2008; Fúster, 2008; Fúster & Campo, 2010; Lunazzi, 2015). Examining the index of any volume of the quarterly journal *Rorschachiana* reveals that it is used on every continent and that research, practice guidelines, and conceptual advances regularly emerge from Europe, South America, and Asia. Within the United States, a specialty literature has examined Rorschach use with its major racial and ethnic groups (e.g., Frank, 1992), although more recent research indicates that ethnicity does not have a large impact on any important Rorschach variables (Meyer, Giromini, Viglione, Reese, & Mihura, 2015). It is a multiculturally fair test.

The contemporary Rorschach is atheoretical. If divorced from its psychoanalytic heritage, what model of personality best fits? Without meaning to be flippant, all of them. Rorschach interpretation can be adapted to nearly any conceptual model or personality theory one likes, ranging from orthodox psychoanalysis to the now-popular five-factor model of personality traits.

Let's be clear on another pressing issue: The Rorschach has critics, and their criticisms need to be taken seriously, rather than simply being dismissed as obsessive academic bickering. For example, Wood, Nezworski, Lilienfeld, and Garb (2003) pointed out that few Rorschach variables are correlated with psychopathological entities such as depression. They were also concerned that people without emotional problems often elevate some of the scores. Awareness of these facts should make us better and more conservative assessors. Yet, the endless academic debates picking at the Rorschach have become trite, often appearing more as attacks than constructive critiques, and are deservedly ignored in clinical practice. One consistent criticism of the Rorschach is the lack of precise meaning to any specific score (i.e., the lack of isomorphic relationships between Rorschach scores and real-life behavior). For example, a person with a markedly elevated CS *WSum6* (Special Scores that are coded when an unusual statement is made) may or may not manifest psychotic thinking, but certainly his or her thinking is significantly more peculiar than that of the typical person. This peculiarity could be attributable to a formal thought disorder or to exceptional creativity. Rorschach score and construct interpretation is more nuanced and hypothesis generative than most textbooks imply.

Within the Rorschach community, the debates over the past decade have been on the evidence-based practice versus practice-based evidence continuum. First, should the Rorschach be a narrow psychological test regularly refined by the findings of psychometric science (e.g., Mihura, Meyer, Dumitrascu, & Bombel, 2013; Tibon Czopp & Zeligman, 2016) or a more flexible, idiographic measure informed by one's experience (Choca, Rossini, & Garside, 2016)? Second, should Rorschach clinicians strictly adhere to one of the two dominant coding systems, or can an eclectic approach be used? And finally, can modifications to the basic administration (e.g., audiotaping, seating) improve the assessment process, or would they render the available norms unusable because of a nonstandardized administration?

What the Rorschach Can Do for You

The Rorschach has been used productively in nearly all evaluative settings. There is a vast literature about its clinical use as an aid in the diagnosis and treatment of psychopathology (see Choca, 2013). Additionally, the use of this test in forensic evaluations has been well documented (Gacono & Evans, 2008), as has its use among "normal" adults in military evaluations, public safety evaluations, industrial–organizational personnel selection evaluations, or religious communities.

As you will see in Chapter 2, there are times when we highly recommend the use of the Rorschach and times when we do not. These recommendations are based on our clinical practice experience. Some clinicians always use the Rorschach regardless of the referral issues or questions. We simply prefer to use it when the referral issue directly engages the strengths of the test.

A Look Into the Future

In our opinion, the Rorschach needs a makeover to remain vital. Resolving the Rorschach's identity crisis and making it briefer and more cost-effective may help save it from extinction. In a later chapter, we introduce several Rorschach modifications that directly address this issue, including Herm, a four-card version of the Rorschach (see Chapter 9). The rest of this book offers a practical way to learn and master the Rorschach.

Getting Started
Tips for Administration

2

When we started graduate school, we were required to purchase our own Rorschach plates. The white casing of these plates was for us a bit like the stethoscope around the neck of medical students, an unmistakable symbol of what was to be our profession, a symbol we carried around with pride. Perhaps disregarding our professor's injunction, we allowed our best friends to take a peek, sometimes in exchange for the promise of serving as our guinea pig—we mean, our practice volunteer—when the time came for us to administer this wonderful tool.

In spite of the decreases in training and clinical utilization (C. Piotrowski, 2015a, 2015b), some of our students become very interested in the Rorschach. Some are just as enthusiastic as we once were about trying their hand with a tool that, in spite of an impressive empirical literature, preserves a bit of the magic and mystery of our clinical world. So, the time has come: You have your practice volunteer, your plates, and your Location sheet, and you are ready to start. But, before you do, let's talk about some issues.

Not all (or perhaps even most) clients referred for psychological evaluations need to be administered the Rorschach. There are both client-based and referral-based reasons to use or not to use this instrument. Both need to be considered.

http://dx.doi.org/10.1037/0000075-003
Assessment Using the Rorschach Inkblot Test, by J. P. Choca and E. D. Rossini

Preadministration Considerations

Since the Rorschach cards rely on visual stimuli, we need to ensure that the individual is able to see the inkblots with reasonable clarity. Color perception needs to be taken into account when interpreting the protocol of color-blind individuals who may give, as a result of their perceptual limitations, less numerous color responses (Malone et al., 2013; Silva, 2002).

We start our contact with an examinee by establishing rapport, giving a brief explanation of what we are about to do, and encouraging the examinee to ask questions. We advise against administering the Rorschach at the very beginning of the evaluation. The reason is that this test may or may not be the most appropriate instrument to use with a particular examinee. If a medical chart or other documents are available, we typically examine those carefully before doing any other work. If the examinee is in the office already, we give the person a self-report questionnaire to complete or an instrument like the Shipley—2 (Shipley, Gruber, Martin, & Klein, 2009) while we are reviewing the documents. Contact with the referral source, whenever possible, is also invaluable in guiding the work we are to perform.

Next, we do a thorough interview. Through this interview, we explore the presenting complaints, the psychosocial stress, the history of emotional problems and treatments (including substance abuse and the family incidence of psychiatric disorders), the medical history, the social and family histories, the educational history, and the occupational history. As the examinee responds to our usually open-ended questions, we observe the person's demeanor and the way in which the person organizes and expresses his or her answers. When necessary, we do a formal mental status examination to ensure the intactness of the cognitive system.

Depending on the referral questions and the issues raised by the documents reviewed or the interview, we decide whether the administration of the Rorschach is warranted. That decision is the first important clinical decision that a Rorschach examiner needs to make. We favor the Rorschach when at least part of the interest involves an area where the Rorschach excels. Such areas include evaluation of the level of energy and productivity, evaluation of the thought process (e.g., the quality of the person's thinking, the effectiveness of mentation, the degree of common sense or personal peculiarities, the reality contact), the interest and empathy the person may have toward others, and the amount of emotional control. The Rorschach may also be useful in cases in which there is malingering potential because it is much harder for the layperson to decide how to respond to this test than to the self-report questionnaires (Ganellen, 2008). It may be indicated when the assessment has clear exploratory aspects, especially using a level of personality organization model. Finally, it may be invaluable when the profiles from the questionnaires are relatively normal but are not consistent with the presenting problems.

Although some work has been done with the Rorschachs of neuropsychologically impaired individuals (e.g., Perry, Potterat, Auslander, Kaplan, & Jeste, 1996), the usual neuropsychological battery does not include the Rorschach. The test may not be useful in routine parenting or child custody evaluations, evaluations of sexual or physical abuse, or evaluations of low-prevalence psychopathologies (e.g., dissociative psycho-pathology). Additional areas that may be better investigated with other instruments include questions about cognitive functions, attention and distractibility, learning disabilities, propensity for addictions, or propensity for suicide or violence or the description of a personality style. Elements of all of these areas may be evident in a particular Rorschach protocol, but there are better instruments to explore those issues. One mistake we see in the Rorschach literature that we blame for much of the criticism the test has received (e.g., Wood, Nezworski, Lilienfeld, & Garb, 2003) has been attempts to use this instrument for purposes for which it is poorly suited.

Rorschach Administration Procedures

In the recent past, the Rorschach has become such an empirical instrument that we have lost much of the clinical richness the instrument used to have (Choca, 2015). For instance, Aronow (Aronow & Reznikoff, 1976; Aronow, Reznikoff, & Moreland, 1994) had a Consensus Rorschach in which he presented the inkblots to an entire family and asked the family members to reach agreement as to what the inkblot looked like. Being less inventive and innovative than Aronow and colleagues, we will describe a more conventional administration. Nevertheless, we aim to recover the Rorschach from those who insist on an obsessive empirical approach, and we encourage a less rigid and more clinically relevant administration.

Administering the Rorschach involves two or three phases (system abbreviations in parentheses indicate the corresponding traditional label): the Free Association (CS) or Response Phase (R-PAS), the Inquiry (CS) or Clarification Phase (R-PAS), and the Follow-Up Phase. The Follow-Up Phase is our own contribution, but it is patterned after the Testing the Limits procedure that Rorschachers developed in the past (Hutt & Shor, 1946; Klopfer, Ainsworth, Klopfer, & Holt, 1954). The procedures or phases are described below.

Deciding on how to introduce and administer the Rorschach is a deceptively challenging task. Both major systems have a standardized instructional text. However, most clinicians modify those instructions to suit their own style. The actual instructions used seem to have had no significant effect on responses either in nonclinical samples (Hartmann, 2001) or among inpatients being treated for substance dependence (Hartmann & Vanem, 2003).

FREE ASSOCIATION OR RESPONSE PHASE

The introduction to the Free Association or Response Phase we use is as follows:

> I am going to show you some inkblots. This is not a test, in the sense that there are no right or wrong answers. People see the world differently, and your responses help me see the world your way. I want you to take a look at each of these cards and tell me what they remind you of [present Card I]. What might this be?

After the individual gives a response, we prompt further response by asking, "What else could this be?" If the individual does not give a second response on the first card, we say, "Most people see more than one thing on these cards; be sure to tell me if you see other things." If the person gives more than one response, the prompt we use is simply, "Anything else?" We continue asking whether there is anything else until we are told there is nothing else.

With consecutive cards, the prompt is, "What might this be?" If the person has not been giving more than one response, we encourage further with the prompt, "What else could this be?" as opposed to the "Anything else?" prompt. We believe these prompts encourage examinees to give us what they would be inclined to give by nature, without intrusively influencing what they would have been inclined to give. To us, the number of responses given is an important piece of data. We do want to encourage the person to share what would come naturally. If the reader wants to follow the R-PAS system instead, however, this system uses the R-Optimized administration procedure that pushes the individual for two responses and pulls the card after four responses on any particular card.

All Rorschach systems recommend verbatim recording of responses. The traditional way was to use paper and pencil to record the responses. Many of us are now using a computer. The Hermann program (Choca, 2017) allows the entering, scoring, and performing of the computations of a Rorschach protocol.[1] Other practitioners type the responses using a word processor. Finally, some practitioners audio record the session after obtaining the appropriate approval.

The Hermann program automatically tracks response times. We do not recommend going back to the stopwatch days of the past, but considering impulsivity or reflectivity, possible behavioral manifestations of editing or defensive censuring, can be valuable.

INQUIRY OR CLARIFICATION PHASE

We introduce the Inquiry or Clarification Phase by saying,

> Now I would like to go through your responses to make sure I understand the way you saw them. For instance, on this card [place Card I on the table so both of you can see it], you were reminded of [read the examinee's first response verbatim, such as "a bird with the wings outstretched"]. Tell me what about the inkblot reminded you of that idea.

After the examinee responds to the above prompt, we ask, "What else about the inkblot helped you to see [put in a brief mention of the response, such as "the bird"]?" Depending on the amount of information we have been getting from the examinee,

---

[1]The Hermann program can be downloaded at http://www.choca-assessments.com.

we may ask instead, "Was there anything else about the inkblot that reminded you of [mentioning here the response]?" We continue to ask the "anything else" question until our examinee tells us that there was nothing else.

Often enough, an examinee is reminded of something else during the Inquiry or Clarification Phase. Depending on your orientation, you may or may not be accepting of those responses. At the very least, you should be noting that such expansion of the original response set took place, because it is certainly saying something about the examinee (see Chapter 4 for more information). We are not inclined to disregard an association just because it was not given at the very first. However, we may use the Follow-Up Phase to learn more about the thought process that led to the additional response. Those of us who score the Rorschach and want to have the benefits of norms must confine ourselves to inquiring or clarifying the response without suggesting ideas or being intrusive.

FOLLOW-UP PHASE

What we call the Follow-Up Phase is an optional phase that allows us to figure out, with fewer restrictions, what the examinee was thinking and the process that may have led to the response obtained. In the case of a sexual response given during the Inquiry Phase, for instance, we may discover that an examinee had seen a penis or a vagina when he or she first saw the card but was too shy to venture into dangerous territory.

In the case of a protocol void of one type of response (e.g., popular, human, color, movement), we use a Testing the Limits procedure (Klopfer et al., 1954). We ask first if the examinee is now reminded of something else in a particular card; then, we focus the person's attention to a particular detail if necessary, suggesting a response if this can be useful (e.g., the humans on Card III, the red blood on Card II), or even tactfully asking why the person may not see what many others see. Testing the Limits is designed to discover how much help we have to give the examinee before the avoided element is obtained or how defensive the person becomes in continuing to avoid the perception. In the case of a response of poor quality, especially in a protocol with good-quality responses, we want to explore the thinking process that led to the poor response.

Finally, when we have a possible insight about what the protocol shows or about a particular response, we may want to check it out with the person so that we can discuss the issue with confidence in our report. One of us recently tested an individual who gave an inordinate number of responses. When this finding was raised during the Follow-Up Phase, the examinee talked about many other hypomanic elements of her life, her extreme electronic multitasking tendencies, her impatience when others don't respond fast enough, and the link between her hypomanic element and the anger management problem that had been the primary presenting complaint. In this case, the Follow-Up Phase findings opened up a whole new area of investigation that served to explain a great deal about this individual, an area that could have been completely missed otherwise.

Closing Comments

Sometimes we have been asked whether we enjoy our diagnostic work or find it boring. If we approach diagnostic work with an interest in collecting the data in a more or less automatic manner, the work can become insufferably tedious. What makes it immensely interesting—at least for some of us—is when we approach the task with the curious eyes of a capable clinician. We would much rather administer only four Rorschach cards (see Chapter 9 for more information) and use the instrument to collaboratively explore what the examinee is all about than administer all 10 cards in a rote and uncreative manner.

Fundamentals of Rorschach Scoring

Understanding the Examinee

3

There is a qualitative exactitude apart from the quantitative. The lack of rigor comes from applying the quantitative method to objects or phenomena that do not require it or accept it.

—*Martin Heidegger*

Clinicians present inkblots, or evocative pictures, or a blank piece of paper on which the examinee is to draw a person under the rain. They look at the response and try to deduce something about the client. To help clinicians make such deductions, scoring systems have been created. Nearly every projective instrument like the Rorschach has a scoring system, a system that a clinician lovingly and carefully designed, and perhaps painfully validated to make the test more "scientific," but that other clinicians have completely disregarded (Rossini & Moretti, 1997).

Most of the inferential work done with projective tests is impressionistic; it resembles a painting by Claude Monet, as opposed to the very detailed work of Jean-Auguste-Dominique Ingres. Projective tests are wonderful clinical instruments but not very good empirical or psychometric tools. The prevailing nomothetic approach to personality psychology in the United States, of compiling statistics across individuals, is what McAdams (1994) called the "psychology of the stranger." In dealing with the totality of a group, McAdams argued, the nomothetic approach describes no one in particular; it misses the sense of the individual's life and the personal meaning of the responses.

The Rorschach is a bit of an exception among the projective instruments in that many clinicians do score the protocol, at least to some degree. Currently

http://dx.doi.org/10.1037/0000075-004
Assessment Using the Rorschach Inkblot Test, by J. P. Choca and E. D. Rossini

there are two competing scoring systems in the United States: the Comprehensive System (CS; Exner, 2003) and the Rorschach Performance Assessment System (R-PAS; Meyer, Viglione, Mihura, Erard, & Erdberg, 2011). Psychologists in other countries have other systems as well. But there has been a significant decline in graduate training on projective techniques (C. Piotrowski, 2015a, 2015b), a diminution that is partly attributable to the difficulty of teaching the Rorschach's intricate scoring and interpretation. In *The Rorschach Clinician*, Potkay (1971) demonstrated that even highly experienced Rorschach assessors answered specific referral questions using remarkably few Rorschach variables, inevitably paired with key demographic variables.

The Basic Rorschach: A Streamlined Scoring System

Borrowing from European clinicians (e.g., Grønnerød & Hartmann, 2010), we propose the Basic Rorschach (BR), a system containing a much smaller number of variables to be scored for every examinee. The BR allows the addition of other variables as appropriate for a specific examinee or circumstances. We propose disregarding, as a matter of routine, variables that typically have a modal frequency of zero and variables that lack interpretive distinctiveness. Our proposal is to routinely score only 33 variables (see Table 3.1). We are proposing a streamlined Rorschach, sort of a Picasso version of the Rorschach—a few line traces that we hope will convey a sense of who the person is. Our attempt to simplify the Rorschach started before the availability of results from the survey on the 'challenges' posed by the learning of the coding (Viglione, Meyer, Resende, & Pignolo, 2017). Our experience, however, and the changes we are proposing, are totally in line with the survey findings. In this chapter, we expand our BR with the more traditional CS and end up with the changes introduced by the R-PAS. Although the table with the BR variables is presented now, the reader may need to look at this table after reviewing the rest of the chapter.

Consider this response to Card I: "a black bird, in flight, with white markings on the spread-out wings." What are the elements of such a response that are important to keep track of? Scoring systems pay attention to 10 areas: Productivity, Location, Perceptual Demand, Determinants, Form Quality, Duplication, Conventionality, Content, Organizational Activity, and Presentation.

The 10 Areas Measured by the Rorschach

PRODUCTIVITY

The person's level of energy and involvement is measured primarily by the number of responses obtained *(R)*, although we also pay attention to the amount of information the examinee gave in the responses. The handling of *R* has been controversial because

TABLE 3.1

Proposed Scoring for the Basic Rorschach

Category	Score codes included
Location	Scored only on the basis of the size of the area: *W*—Use of the whole inkblot *D*—Large detail; any area larger than approximately 10% of the inkblot *d*—Small detail; any area smaller than approximately 10% of the inkblot *S*—Use of white space; significant reversal of the figure–ground perspective
Determinants	*M*—Human movement; without the active or passive indicators *FM*—Animal movement; without the active or passive indicators *m*—Inanimate movement; without the active or passive indicators *FC*—Form-dominant color response based on content *CF*—Color-dominant form response based on content *C*—Color response with no form *C'*—Any achromatic response *Y*—Any shading response *T*—Any texture response *F*—Response with no other Determinant
Popular	*P*—Popular response; nine possible, based on just Content and Location; no *P* for Card IX
Form quality	Scored based entirely on the examiner's judgment: *o*—Ordinary; content reasonably consistent with the shape of the inkblot *u*—Unusual; content marginally consistent with the shape of the inkblot *– *—Content not consistent with the shape of the inkblot
Content	*H*—Human content; includes *Hd*, human detail or incomplete human figure *(H)*—Fictionalized human content; includes *(Hd)*, imaginary or fictional human detail *A*—Animal content; includes *Ad*, animal detail or incomplete animal form *(A)*—Fictionalized animal content; includes *(Ad)*, imaginary or fictional animal detail *An*—Anatomy; includes *Xy*, X-ray *Sx*—Sexual content *Bl*—Blood *Na*—Nature; includes *Bt*, botany *Cg*—Clothing *Fd*—Food *Cl*—Cloud *Ge*—Geography; includes *Ls*, landscape *Fi*—Fire; includes *Ex*, explosion *Ob*—Human-made object; includes *Art*, object of art; *Ay*, anthropology; *Sc*, science; and *Hh*, household object
Pathological verbalization	*PV*—Any bizarre statement; includes Special Scores or Cognitive Codes (Level 1 statements are disregarded.)
Other	*NB*—Nota bene to flag any other aspect that needs attention

the length of the protocol will inevitably influence the other score categories, and the different systems take different approaches. The BR and the CS allow Productivity to vary freely, except that the CS rejects protocols with fewer than 14 responses. The R-PAS uses *prompts and pulls*, a system that pushes the examinee to give at least two responses per card but pulls the card after the fourth response. The issue is whether the system emphasizes the discovery of what the examinee will do by nature or standardization of the results.

LOCATION

The Location score tracks the section of the inkblot used for the response. *W* indicates a response that uses the whole inkblot. The assignment of *D* for large detail is more complicated for both the CS and R-PAS. Both of these systems contaminate the size of the area with the predominance of its use: The area not only has to be reasonably large, but it also has to be an obvious area, one that sticks out. The addition of two *D* areas in a response is still considered a *D*. Unfortunately, the only way to tell if an area qualifies for a *D* in those systems is to look the area up in a Location chart. The BR proposal is to separate the issues of size and predominance. We propose using *D* for any area that uses 10% of the inkblot or more.

The CS and R-PAS code for small areas, or areas that are not commonly used, is *Dd*. Although many *Dd* areas are noted in the Location charts, the *Dd* designation can be used for any area that does not appear in the chart. We propose abandoning the *Dd* designation and using a lowercase *d* for any area that is less than 10% of the inkblot.

Finally, the use of white space is coded as *S*. The R-PAS distinguishes between a complete reversal of the figure–ground perspective (*SR*; e.g., the white jet in the center portion of Card II) and the use of white space in an integrated fashion *(SI)* to complement a response that does not reverse the usual perspective (e.g., the eyes and mouth of a mask on Card I). We propose to use *S* only in the case of a complete figure–ground reversal and no coding for an integrated use of the white space.

PERCEPTUAL DEMAND

Exner (2003) used Developmental Quality *(DQ)* in the CS to assess the Perceptual Demand the response makes on the shape of the inkblot. The *DQ* score is complicated, has generally not been shown to be of much interpretive value, and is often ignored by practitioners. The R-PAS combines this concept with Organizational Activity into Object Quality: Synthesis *(Sy)* is scored when there are two separate, distinct objects in a relationship (e.g., two people washing clothes in Card III), and vagueness *(Vg)* is scored when the outline or boundaries are indistinct (e.g., blood in Card II). For the BR, we propose abandoning consideration of both the Perceptual Demand and the somewhat related Organizational Activity.

DETERMINANTS

The Determinant codes characterize the elements of the inkblot that evoked the response. The most basic Determinant is the shape or form of the inkblot *(F)*. Other Determinants include movement, shading, perspective, and color. Also considered Determinants by both the CS and R-PAS are reflections, such as a person looking at a mirror on Card II. Reflections are coded *Fr* and *rF* by the CS and *r* by the R-PAS. As Hellmut Brinkmann (personal communication, 2015) has pointed out, seeing the same figure on both sides of a symmetrical construction does not address the issue of what element of the inkblot evoked the response and should not be considered a Determinant. Pairs, represented by the symbol *(2)*, are considered separately from the Determinants in the CS and are considered an Object Quality by the R-PAS. The BR does not score reflections or doubles because any *D* or *d* perceptions seen on one side are likely to have a similar perception on the other. Moreover, both reflections and doubles are of unclear interpretive meaning.

Form *(F)* is scored only when there are no other Determinants. Traditionally, Rorschach practitioners computed Lambda, the proportion of *F* to non-*F* responses ($L = F / R - F$). Note that this is not the same as the proportion of *F* responses (F / R) or the *F* percent ($[F / R] * 100$). Lambda is an old-fashioned label, and because it is confusing, we don't often use it. Except for *F*, all other Determinants that can be scored for a response are entered in the score string. A response that has more than one Determinant is called a *blend*. The different Determinants in a blend are separated by a period (CS) or a comma (R-PAS). The Determinants in a blend are listed in a conventional order (i.e., movement, color, achromatic color, shading, dimension, reflection; e.g., people dancing at a party with red decorations on Card III would be *Ma.CF*). Chapter 5 covers blends in more detail.

Movement is the one Determinant that is a complete projection because inkblots are stationary. There are three kinds of movement: human movement *(M)*, animal movement *(FM)*, and inanimate movement *(m)*. Movement responses can be further classified as active *(a)* or passive *(p)*; this element is typically added to the primary code (i.e., *Ma* or *Mp*, *FMa* or *FMp*, *ma* or *mp*). *Active movement* is defined as any action that implies more movement than a smile, and *passive movement* is any action with less movement than a smile. Yet, even with this simple active–passive definition, the coding decision can be challenging in practice (Holaday, 1998). Moreover, the great majority of movement responses are of the active variety, and the interpretive meaning of the active–passive distinction is not well supported by the literature. Consequently, no active–passive distinction is made in BR.

Color can be chromatic, denoted by *C*, or achromatic, denoted by *C'*. An important aspect of the chromatic color response is the relative prominence the form of the inkblot plays in the response. That prominence is decided by taking the Content into consideration. A red butterfly has a very definite shape, and the form is a prevalent part of the perception; such prominence is noted by coding the *F* first *(FC)*. In contrast, the shape of fireworks is indefinite; here, the form is less important than the color, and the *C* of the color is placed first *(CF)*. Finally, there are color responses with no form, as when the color reminds the examinee of happiness; such responses are scored with a *C* by itself with no *F*. When more than one color Determinant needs to be scored for a response, only the code that is the least form dominant is used (e.g., a clown with a red hat *[FC]* on Card II stepping on a pool of blood *[CF]* would be scored *CF*). Color blindness obviously drastically complicates the assessment of a Rorschach protocol.

The CS follows the same logic and distinctions of the above paragraph for achromatic responses (e.g., a black bat on Card V *[FC']*, a dark cloud on Card VII *[C'F]*, and depression on Card IV *[C']*). Similarly, those considerations are followed for responses including texture (*T*; e.g., a furry animal pelt on Card VI) with scores *FT, TF,* or *T*; vista *(V)* responses (e.g., islands seen from above on Card VII) with scores *FV* or *VF*; and diffuse shading (*Y*; e.g., an x-ray because of the shading on Card IV) with scores *FY* or *YF*. The BR and R-PAS do not distinguish the relative importance of the form with noncolor responses, and would simply score the letter without the *F—C', T, V,* or *Y*. Both the CS and R-PAS recognize dimension *(FD)* when the outline evokes a sense of perspective (e.g., the giant seen from below on Card IV because the feet are much larger than the head, an animal behind a bush on Card IX). The BR does not have a score for dimension.

FORM QUALITY

Form Quality *(FQ)* is arguably the most important aspect of a Rorschach response because the quality of the thinking process is typically not revealed well by other instruments. Form Quality addresses reality-testing capacity in visual perception, or the goodness-of-fit: whether the response is consistent with the shape on the inkblot. Both the CS and R-PAS unfortunately contaminate the issues of frequency and accuracy. Although the CS recognizes a response of superior Form Quality *(FQ+)*, this determination has mostly been abandoned.

Ordinary Form Quality *(FQo)* is given to a response that is relatively frequent and can be clearly seen, such as a bat on Card V. Unusual Form Quality *(FQu)* is assigned to a response that is either infrequent or cannot easily be seen (e.g., humans leaning on each other back to back on Card V). Minus Form Quality *(FQ–)* denotes an infrequent or inaccurate response (e.g., a skeleton on Card V).

From the perspective of how well the response adheres to the shape of the inkblot, some responses are obviously of good quality and some responses are terrible. The determination of the Form Quality becomes an issue only with a marginal response that could perhaps be seen as acceptable by one practitioner and not acceptable by another. Both the CS and R-PAS offer extensive tables with a myriad of responses and the recommended Form Quality. Obviously, no table can include an exhaustive list of all possible responses, and both the CS and R-PAS offer suggestions for deciding on responses not included in the table. When all is said and done, however, this matter must be left to the clinician's judgment. One asset of the Rorschach is that any aspect of importance will repeat itself: If there is only one response that is of questionable Form Quality, the score given will not matter; if there are several responses of this kind, the finding is interpretable regardless of the score. With BR, we propose letting the clinician make the judgment from the start, without looking anything up on a table.

DUPLICATION

Many examinees acknowledge the symmetry of the inkblots by seeing a reflection or by speaking of two similar objects. The reflection score has already been described because both the CS and R-PAS include this attribute as a Determinant. Duplication involves pairs (e.g., seeing two animals, one on each side of Card VIII), coded as *(2)*. The BR proposes to disregard both reflection and pairs, mostly because of the lack of interpretive usefulness.

CONVENTIONALITY

Popular responses *(P)* are responses given to a particular card in a third of protocols or more. The *P* designation is dictated mostly by the content of the response, but it goes across categories because it requires a particular location. Many Popular responses occur much more frequently than once in every three protocols; for example, the four-legged animal on the side of Card VIII is seen by 90% of examinees. Only one *P* can be scored on a card. If the examinee gives more than one response that would qualify, only the first of those responses is designated a *P* because the second response would invariably be a variance on the same idea. Table 3.2 lists the responses recognized as Populars.

CONTENT

The CS recognizes 27 Content categories. Some of these categories are seldom used, and the interpretive meaning of most of these categories is unclear. The number of categories was reduced for the BR and the R-PAS. Table 3.3 shows the symbol used

TABLE 3.2

Popular Responses

Card	Location	Response
I	*W*	Bat or butterfly
II	Black *D*	Animal
III	Black *D*	Human or humanlike figure
IV	*W* or *D7*	Human or humanlike figure
V	*W*	Bat or butterfly
VI	*W* or *D1*	Animal skin
VII	*D9*	Human head
VIII	*D1*	Animal
IX	*D3*	Human or humanlike figure
X	*D1*	Crab or spider

Note. Numbers with *D* are from a Location table provided in the test manual.

TABLE 3.3

Content Codes Included in Three Rorschach Scoring Systems

Code	Name	Scoring system		
		BR	**CS**	**R-PAS**
H	Whole human	✓	✓	✓
(H)	Imaginary or fictional whole human	✓	✓	✓
Hd	Human detail or incomplete human figure		✓	✓
(Hd)	Imaginary or fictional human detail		✓	✓
Hx	Human experience such as emotion		✓	
A	Whole animal	✓	✓	✓
(A)	Imaginary or fictional whole animal	✓	✓	✓
Ad	Animal detail or incomplete animal form		✓	✓
(Ad)	Imaginary or fictional animal detail		✓	✓
An	Anatomy; internal body parts not visible from outside	✓	✓	✓
Art	Objects of art such as paintings or decorative objects		✓	✓
Ay	Anthropology; objects with historical or cultural import		✓	✓
Bl	Blood	✓	✓	✓
Bt	Botany or plants; skip if nature *(Na)* is scored		✓	
Cg	Clothing	✓	✓	✓
Cl	Clouds	✓	✓	
Ex	Explosion		✓	✓
Fi	Fire	✓	✓	✓
Fd	Food	✓	✓	
Ge	Geography, such as a map	✓	✓	
Hh	Household object		✓	
Ob	Object; includes any human-made object except clothing *(Cg)*	✓		
Ls	Landscape; skip if nature *(Na)* is scored		✓	
Na	Nature	✓	✓	
Sc	Science		✓	
Sx	Sexual organs or activity or sexy clothing	✓	✓	✓
Xy	X-ray		✓	
Idio	Content not classified in other categories		✓	
Nc	Content not classified in other categories			✓
Total		14	27	17

Note. BR = Basic Rorschach; CS = Comprehensive System; R-PAS = Rorschach Performance Assessment System.

for the different categories; the last three columns show the system that uses each symbol. For specific coding criteria, the user is referred to the CS or R-PAS manual.

For human and animal responses, both the CS and R-PAS make three scoring distinctions. These systems distinguish between a response that involves the entire figure, *H* or *A*; a response that involves part of the figure, *Hd* or *Ad*; and a response that involves a figure that is not quite real, in which case the symbol is put in parentheses: *(H)*, *(Hd)*, *(A)*, or *(Ad)*. Examples of fantasized figures may be a cartoon character, Godzilla, or a unicorn. The end result is that both CS and R-PAS have four different scoring categories each for human and animal responses. For us, the tendency to see wholes or parts is already addressed with the manner of approach (Location), and we are not impressed with the interpretive distinctiveness between *H* and *Hd* or *A* and *Ad*. Consequently, the proposal for the BR is to distinguish only between the real and the fantasized perception.

ORGANIZATIONAL ACTIVITY

The CS uses one variable (Z score) to take into account the effort that was necessary to produce the response. This variable (see Chapter 4) is not one that is used by most clinicians.

PRESENTATION

As part of a response, or in addition to the response, an examinee may offer comments that are revealing and interpretable. Such comments are part of Presentation, referred to as *Special Scores* in the CS and *Cognitive Codes* in the R-PAS. A distinction is made between a remark that does not reveal a great deal of pathology (Level 1) and a more pathological presentation (Level 2). We always have trouble deciding exactly how to code one of these comments. As a result, the BR groups all Level 2 comments together as a pathological verbalization *(PV)* and disregards Level 1 comments. The R-PAS distinguishes between Cognitive Codes that are of a language and reasoning nature *(DV, DR, and PEC)*, perceptual nature *(INC, FAB, and CON)*, or thematic nature *(ABS, PER, COP, MAH, MAP, AGM, AGC, MOR, and ODL)*. Table 3.4 lists the Presentation codes used by the CS and R-PAS.

TABLE 3.4

Special Scores or Cognitive Codes

Code	Name	Explanation
DV1	Deviant Verbalization, Level 1	Mistaken or inappropriate word (e.g., a pair of two birds)
DV2	Deviant Verbalization, Level 2	Mistake leading to failure of communication (e.g., an extraneous virgin bird)
DR1	Deviant Response, Level 1	Task distortions (e.g., I was hoping to see a butterfly)

(continues)

TABLE 3.4 (*Continued*)

Special Scores or Cognitive Codes

Code	Name	Explanation
DR2	Deviant Response, Level 2	Task distortions showing loose associations or incomprehensible explanations (e.g., an angry monster, it may hurt me, I don't want to see it anymore)
ALOG (CS)	Alogic	Confused thinking used spontaneously to justify a response (e.g., this must be a head of lettuce because it is right next to the rabbit)
PEC (R-PAS)	Peculiar Logic	
INC1	Incongruous Combination, Level 1	Implausible attributes (e.g., a four-legged chicken)
INC2	Incongruous Combination, Level 2	Illogical and bizarre attributes (e.g., a germ dancing the polka)
FAB1	Fabulized Combination, Level 1	Implausible relationship (e.g., two chickens playing basketball)
FAB2	Fabulized Combination, Level 2	Implausible and bizarre relationship (e.g., a heart pumping blood into a submarine)
CON	Contamination	Two impressions fused into a single response (e.g., the face of a snake alligator)
ABS	Abstract Representation	Response involving an abstraction (e.g., happiness)
PER	Personal Knowledge	Use of a personal experience to justify the response (e.g., I know this is a bat because I have been to the zoo and I have seen one just like it)
COP	Cooperative Movement	Positive, pleasant interaction between two objects (e.g., two waiters setting a table)
MOR	Morbid Content	Object that is damaged, distressed, dysphoric (e.g., a dead animal). Note: The *MOR* does not imply the action of another.
MAH (R-PAS)	Mutuality of Autonomy—Health	Objects autonomously engaged in reciprocal interaction (e.g., two people singing a duet)
MAP (R-PAS)	Mutuality of Autonomy—Pathology	Object that intentionally compromises the autonomy or integrity of another (e.g., a smashed bug)
AG (CS)	Aggressive Movement	Hostile activity or intent (e.g., a person being ripped apart by wolves)
AGM (R-PAS)		
AGC (R-PAS)	Aggressive Content	Involving an aggressive, dangerous, harmful, injurious, malevolent, or predatory element (e.g., gun, dangerous animal or animal part)
ODL (R-PAS)	Oral Dependent Language	Oral activity or interpersonal passivity and dependence (e.g., eating, belly, kiss, talk, begging, praying)

Concluding Remarks

Frank J. Kobler (1983), the professor who taught the Rorschach to both of us at Loyola University Chicago, asserted that the aim of the Rorschach was not to "measure" but to "understand" the examinee (p. 136). Scoring the Rorschach is useful if the scoring highlights different aspects of the individual that could have been missed otherwise. By describing the different scores, we aimed in this chapter to summarize the elements of the test that clinicians should be aware of. The reader will have to judge the extent to which the more intricate CS and R-PAS scoring systems are superior—in helping us understand the individual—to the simpler BR scoring system we are proposing.

Scoring and Interpreting Individual Variables

4

People like to use maps when traveling. Someone's directions to the restaurant (turn right, walk two blocks, turn left . . .) will get us there, but leave us sort of lost. We are inside the maze and would benefit from having a sense of what the maze looks like from above. It is when we look at the map that we see why we had to turn right instead of left. We can get to the restaurant without the map, but we need the map to truly know where we were going.

The Rorschach map is the Structural Summary. The Structural Summary contains the sums of all the single variables as well as numerous ratios, indices, and constellations in an examinee's protocol. We do not advocate investing a great deal of effort in formulating the "right" score for a response, and we see the Structural Summary as containing ballpark figures. It is like one of those free maps one gets at a hotel that does not have all of the streets but shows the points of interest. It is a useful overview, a sketch that ensures clinicians will not miss a dominant issue when they interpret the protocol. This chapter reviews the basic Structural Summary, and Chapter 5 covers the relationships of scores and the more complex derivatives. The Structural Summary is time consuming and cumbersome to create by hand, but there are programs, such as Hermann[1] (Choca, 2017), that can help with the task.

---

[1]The Hermann program can be downloaded at http://www.choca-assessments.com.

http://dx.doi.org/10.1037/0000075-005
Assessment Using the Rorschach Inkblot Test, by J. P. Choca and E. D. Rossini

Most Rorschach evaluations compare the scores of a particular examinee to community norms, such as the norms Exner published through the years (e.g., Exner, 1993, 2003, 2007). More recent international community norms from a multitude of countries were published in a supplement to the *Journal of Personality Assessment* (Meyer, Erdberg, & Shaffer, 2007), and there are norms for the R-PAS (Meyer, Viglione, Mihura, Erard, & Erdberg, 2011). Selecting which norms to use will be the first interpretive question you need to decide.

The comparison group used for norms has varied for different instruments. Like the Rorschach, several other clinical tools were standardized with nonpsychiatric community samples, notably the Minnesota Multiphasic Personality Inventory—2 (MMPI–2; Butcher, Dahlstrom, Graham, Tellegen, & Kaemmer, 1989). Some instruments, such as the Millon Clinical Multiaxial Inventory (Millon, 2016), were standardized with a psychiatric sample. Finally, there are tests that have both community and psychiatric norms, such as the Personality Assessment Inventory (Morey, 1991). We think comparing an individual to both community and psychiatric norms is useful for understanding the person.

We and our colleagues did a meta-analysis of published CS community norms that included both Exner's and the international norms (Muñoz, Choca, Rossini, & Garside, 2011). We also performed a meta-analysis of psychiatric norms that included the Exner psychiatric data and an additional 960 clinical protocols we collected. Finally, a comparison between the two meta-analyses is also available.[2]

To determine what to interpret using the Structural Summary, the clinician notes what values for the examinee are outside the expected range. The cutoff for the determination of lows and highs is arbitrary. We use 1.5 standard deviations above or below the mean because it is the cutoff used by many of the personality questionnaires, such as the MMPI–2. For a normally distributed score, that cutoff would leave 86% of the population in the acceptable range, with 7% being high and 7% being low. We use the term *marker* for any score that is outside the expected range. Thus, a marker is a score that is of clinical interest.

Our interpretive approach is based on the premise that no marker is necessarily indicative of a specific attribute. A particular marker may be revealing different things for different people (see, e.g., the text box for Productivity). The clinician's job is to understand the person, to play detective, to ask questions, to test out the different hypotheses in order to develop a sense of what the marker means for that person. The suggestions in our text boxes should not be seen as definitive or exhaustive, and the suggestions may be relevant in isolation or in combination with another suggestion.

To understand the person, clinicians need to go beyond the cutoffs and the markers. Chapters 6 and 7 are designed to help the reader go beyond the markers. Moreover, it is useful in reports to highlight the positives as well as the negatives. Sometimes the positives are distilled from Rorschach scores that are within the expected range. Such may be the case, for instance, with an individual whose Rorschach showed a reasonable Form Quality level and a lack of Special Scores or Cognitive Codes. A balance in the manner of approach or in the emotional reaction may be worth noting.

---

[2]All of this material can be found online at http://pubs.apa.org/books/supp/choca.

Important Considerations for Understanding Markers

To fully understand a marker, clinicians have to consider three important issues. First, they have to develop a sense of what the marker reveals about the person's mode of operation. For instance, people with a high *R* marker, or a protocol that has more responses than expected, may be inventive and animated in real life. These people may be driven and highly motivated. However, their energy level may be excessive, and they may be too talkative, intrusive, or disorganized to be effective. The protocol may show the inclination to repeat the same ideas, a perseverative tendency that may also be seen in the person's daily life. How well the Rorschach responses are explained by the individual may offer an indication of how adaptive this particular attribute may be. In any event, clinicians can generalize from the Rorschach marker to describe how the individual appears on the surface and what strategies he or she uses in order to function.

Second, clinicians can investigate the level below the surface. Perhaps with the help of Follow-Up Phase questions, they can explore what is fueling the mode of operation suggested by the marker. This addresses motivation. One could say, "You gave more responses than most people; what do you suppose that means?" The high *R* marker may indicate a wish to please, or a wish to appear gifted and competent, or an obsessive–compulsive need to examine all parts of the inkblot, or a high adrenaline drive that pushed the person to go on, or a misunderstanding of the instructions leading to a string of free associations, or something else. If clinicians have an intuition, they can use prompts to check the intuition out: for example, "Some people give a lot of responses because _____. Do you suppose that is what was going on with you?" As clinicians listen to what examinees say, they are "exploding" the hotel map to see the buildings, and they are developing a better understanding of what the person is all about.

Third, the clinician can explore how well the finding generalizes to real life. The premise of the Rorschach is that how a person responds to the inkblots is how he or she responds in the real world. What impact does the high energy level have on the person's functioning? As with any psychological trait, high energy has advantages and disadvantages. Can the person discuss the pluses and the minuses, or the possibility of adjusting this particular trait to the needs of the situation? This third level may be part of the feedback session rather than done when the Rorschach is administered. Such a recommendation would be consistent with the trend toward using a collaborative/therapeutic assessment model of interactive testing and feedback (Finn, Fischer, & Handler, 2012).

Interpreting Individual Markers

With those three important considerations in mind, let's look at individual measures. In this section, we offer possible interpretations for low and high scores, including research findings that correlate specific thought processes, personality types, and behavioral patterns with these scores. In the text boxes below, the first cutoff in the parentheses is derived from our unpublished meta-analysis of the community samples, whereas the second comes from our unpublished psychiatric meta-analysis; both were derived using 1.5 standard deviations from the mean. In the many cases in which the low cutoff (the mean of the meta-analysis minus 1.5 standard deviations) was close to zero, we don't provide a cutoff value and have a dash (–) instead. In such cases we advise the reader that a low score is uninterpretable. N/A (not available) is used when no information was available from a meta-analysis.

PRODUCTIVITY

People vary in the amount of energy they have at their disposal. There are people with a turbo engine: They have all sorts of ideas when they look at the inkblots and are reminded of a multitude of things. Other people are more thoughtful and restrained, wanting to make sure they have something to contribute before they speak up. Still others have trouble coming up with anything. People also vary in the amount of energy they invest in the evaluation. The number of Rorschach responses—indicated by *R*—is an important piece of information that invariably reveals something about the examinee.

Possible Interpretations for Response *(R)* Markers

Low scores (< 11, < 10): The examinee
- Has low intellectual capacity or low expressive vocabulary, especially for nonnative speakers of English
- Has low motivation
- With high *F*, has constriction of psychological functioning so that the individual is guarded and unproductive; is overcontrolled
- Is defensive; fears disclosure; shows a passive–aggressive approach to the testing, perhaps to life; is resistant; possibly has the intent to avoid the task; displays oppositional negativism
- Is distrustful, suspicious, paranoid
- Is depressed; has difficulty becoming energized and motivated

High scores (> 34, > 33): The examinee
- Is intelligent
- Has high motivation and good resources. However, consideration has to be given to the quality of the responses. Evaluate the protocol for the richness of Determinants and Contents. Some protocols have a high *R* because of perseverative repetition of the same responses.
- Has an obsessive–compulsive need for completeness
- Is expansive, inclined to overproduction; is overeager in committing to the task
- Is trusting; wishes to be cooperative and perform well
- Has a strong achievement drive
- Displays a manic or hypomanic state; has difficulty limiting interactions with the world

High scores have been associated with extraversion and show-off tendencies.

LOCATION

Impressionist painters like Claude Monet created a new and unique vision of a situation in which the colors and broad strokes took precedence over lines and contours. Their interest was not in the fine details. In contrast, classical and neoclassical painters such as Jean-August-Dominique Ingres paid very careful attention to details, down to the folds of a dress. As clinicians look around, they observe both kinds of people. There are those who are visionaries; they want to consider the entire situation, the "forest," the purpose of some action, the *what* and the *why*. Other people are more interested in the details. These people want to consider the "trees," the bark of the trees, the leaves; they want to carefully assemble the *how*. For the president of a company, one may want the visionary, a person who views the whole playing field, even at the expense of overlooking details. For an accountant, one wants the compulsive individual, the detail person who is going to check everything twice. Of course, most people are balanced with regard to this attribute, having an eye for both the macro and the micro view. There is something to be said for having all types of thinkers. The Rorschach gets to the forest-or-trees issue with the classification of the Locations used for the response. Figure 4.1 shows the frequency of the different Locations in the average protocol.

To give a whole response, the examinee has to look at the entire inkblot and integrate all of the parts into the response. The first four Location scores are interdependent: The higher the proportion of whole *(W)* responses an examinee gives, the lower the proportion of detailed responses *(D, Dd,* and *d)* possible. Cards I, IV, and V easily generate whole responses; some effort is required to provide whole responses for Cards II, VI, VII, and VIII; and it is difficult to give whole responses to Cards III, IX, and X. Detailed areas are easy to distinguish on every card except Card V. Responses

FIGURE 4.1

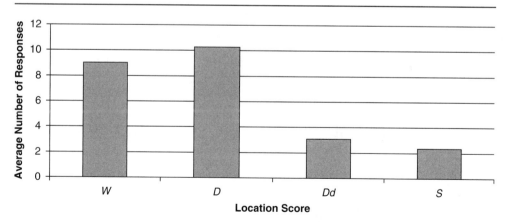

Frequency of the different locations in the average protocol. Data were taken from our unpublished meta-analysis of community samples. *W* = use of the whole inkblot; *D* = large detail; *Dd* = small or unusual detail; *S* = use of white space.

using white space *(S)* are most commonly given in the first three cards. Cards II and VII (the latter with the card upside-down) are the most likely to elicit figure–ground reversals.

Possible Interpretations for Whole Inkblot *(W)* Markers

Low scores (< 3, < 2): The examinee
- Is unable to see the entire picture
- Is easily pulled into the practical but unable to integrate the details into an overview
- Has trouble accepting ambiguity
- Is perfectionistic (rejects *W* perception because it is not precisely correct)

High scores (> 15, > 15): The examinee
- Is a holistic thinker; strives to organize to an excessive degree
- Is overly ambitious
- Makes more effort than usual to integrate the world into a holistic view
- Has trouble seeing the practical, the easy answers, the actions that can be taken in an economical manner
- With a low *R* score, is superficial, possibly casual about tasks, and unconcerned about the complexities in life

---

Possible Interpretations of Large Detail *(D)* Markers

Low scores (< 3, < 1): The examinee
- Is impractical
- Does not take advantage of easily accomplishable tasks
- May tend to work harder at a task than necessary

High scores (> 18, > 18): The examinee
- Tends to emphasize the practical, easy solutions; is economical; has an "it-is-what-it-is" style
- Is likely to miss the overall picture

If *R* is high, the high *D* may just be attributable to the pressure to give responses.

Possible Interpretations for Small Detail *(Dd)* Markers

Low scores: Not interpretable

High scores (> 8, > 9):
With high *R*, high *Dd* probably results from the high energy level and involvement, and not from the other possible causes given below.

The examinee
- With high *S*, is negativistic, oppositional
- Holds a micro view of the environment, a view that stresses the minutiae or details at the expense of seeing the global picture

- Has an obsessive–compulsive and perfectionistic approach to life
- Is peculiar or unique, inclined to look at the world in a way that is different from the way others see it
- Is guarded or mistrustful; tries to minimize ambiguities
- Is impractical; has difficulty recognizing the obvious

Possible Interpretations for Small Detail *(d)* Markers (Less Than 10% of Inkblot)

Low scores: Not interpretable

High scores (N/A): The examinee
- Holds a micro view of the environment, a view that stresses the minutiae or details at the expense of seeing the global picture
- Has an obsessive–compulsive and perfectionistic approach to life
- Is guarded or mistrustful; tries to minimize ambiguities
- Is impractical; has difficulty recognizing the obvious

Possible Interpretations for White Space *(S)* Markers

Low scores: Not interpretable

High scores (> 5, > 5): The examinee
- Engages in negativism
- Has an oppositional tendency; is rebellious (except Mihura, Meyer, Dumitrascu, & Bombel's, 2013, meta-analysis did not find support for this variable as an indicator of an oppositional tendency)
- Wishes to look at the world in a way that is different from the way it is presented and the way most people see it. This tendency may be an asset or a liability depending on how it is used by the individual.
- Has difficulty sustaining relationships because of the inclination to be contradictory; is intolerant of the usual social compromises

High scores have been associated with lower response quality and unconventionality. High scores have been associated with a more complex perception of the environment.

PERCEPTUAL DEMAND

Developmental Quality *(DQ)* represents an attempt to quantify the amount of form or visual structure that is demanded by a particular response. In our mind, this construct is redundant with some Determinants. For instance, responses like blood, fire, or foliage have little form demand but call for Determinants that note the minimization of the form demand (e.g., *CF* instead of *FC*). A response that makes a reference to fire because of the color of Card IX, for instance, does not have a high form requirement and would be scored *CF* (as opposed to *FC*) as a result. We are not sure why we need another score, the vague Developmental Quality *(DQ = v)*, to account for the same phenomenon.

Moreover, much work had to be done to extricate the Developmental Quality from the Form Quality ratings (Exner, 2003). Finally, we now know that the amount of form used by the examinee is mostly related to the intellectual and perceptual ability of the individual (e.g., S. R. Smith, Bistis, Zahka, & Blais, 2007; Wood, Krishnamurthy, & Archer, 2003). Given these considerations, we do not attach much significance to this score, and we don't use it.

DETERMINANTS

The core of the Rorschach Structural Summary are the Determinants. The Determinants reflect the visual–perceptual aspects of the inkblots that were used for the response.

The highest bar of the psychogram in Figure 4.2 shows the frequency of the responses formulated on the basis of only the shape of the inkblot. These *F* responses are associations without embellishments, responses that include only the elements that are minimally required for a Rorschach response. Tests administered without an appropriate amount of encouragement or administrations that are rushed on the part of either the examiner or examinee lead to high *F* markers. Because of this element, it is best to consider an abbreviated Rorschach like our four-card Herm (see Chapter 9) than a poorly administered full Rorschach. As the frequency of *F* diminishes, the bars on either side of the psychogram must come up.

On the left side of the psychogram are the movement, texture, vista, and shading responses. Responses with such scores represent the individual's internal psychic

FIGURE 4.2

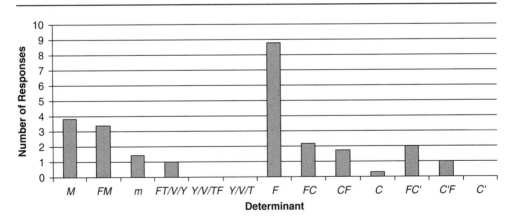

Distribution of determinants in the average protocol. Data were taken from our unpublished meta-analysis of community samples. *M* = human movement; *FM* = animal movement; *m* = inanimate movement; *FT/V/Y* = *FT* + *FV* + *FY*; *Y/V/TF* = *YF* + *VT* + *TF*; *Y/V/T* = *Y* + *V* + *T*; *F* = response with no other Determinant; *FC* = form-dominant color response based on content; *CF* = color-dominant form response based on content; *C* = color response with no form; *FC'* = form dominant achromatic color response based on content; *C'F* = achromatic color dominant form response based on content; *C'* = achromatic color response with no form.

resources in that these elements are not visually predominant on the inkblot. These Determinants mostly involve a creation on the part of the examinee, a fabrication coming from the inside the person, as opposed to something evoked by a prominent aspect of the inkblot. The right side of the psychogram shows the frequency of responses based on color, an element that is clearly part of the inkblot. Because the color Determinants are evoked by external material, they are likely to reflect the person's response to the outside world. The association of color and emotion means that the color Determinants speak of the person's emotional response to the environment.

In the sections that follow, we focus on the center *F* bar of Figure 4.2 first. Then, using the conventional order dictated by prevalence and importance, an order also followed in Chapter 3, we consider movement on the left side of the psychogram, color on the right side, and then the rest of the Determinants.

Form

The proportion of form or shape *(F)* responses is an important variable, an index of the psychological willingness to become involved with ambiguous stimuli, and an index of the person's control. People with a high *F* bar are like Sergeant Joe Friday or Mr. Spock: Just the facts, please. In contrast, people with a low *F* bar are more psychologically complex because they routinely access fantasy or emotions and add spice to their view of the world.

Possible Interpretations for Form or Shape *(F)* Markers

Low scores (< 2, < 2): The examinee
- Looks at the world in an overly complex manner
- Is involved with stimuli to the extent that the affect disrupts the person's cognitive functions
- May be excessively open and revealing, without enough ability to inhibit impulses
- Has inadequate control over emotions or inner feelings; is often a victim of own needs and conflicts
- Is unable to take a detached position or ignore elements in order to focus on the most important aspect
- Has difficulty maintaining satisfactory interpersonal relationships

High scores (> 16, > 19): The examinee
- Looks at the world simplistically; does not notice or articulate subtleties of both the external and internal environment; is unreflective (seen more with children [Exner, Thomas, & Mason, 1985], with children with attention-deficit/hyperactivity disorder [Strickland, 2006; Zhong, Jing, Wang, & Yin, 2007], and with individuals with closed head injuries [Exner, Colligan, Boll, Stischer, & Hillman, 1996])
- Is conservative in dealing with the self and the environment
- Is overcontrolled, constricted, insecure, fearful of involvement
- Is unimaginative
- Is uninvolved
- Is defensive and guarded, especially if *R* is low, not wanting to take a risk at revealing much about himself or herself; seen with defensive forensic criminals (e.g., Conti, 2007)

Movement

Movement responses reveal part of one's inner world and appear on the left side of the psychogram. Movement responses involve the injection of action into the response and consequently have an energy or dynamism that is not present in other responses. It adds something to the response that is not there on the card.

The three types of movement (human, animal, and inanimate) reflect very different inner worlds. Human movement *(M)* increases dramatically with age, and the frequency of animal movement *(FM)* shows a small decrease. The net effect is that the proportion of *M* to *FM* changes so that, with adults, more human movement is expected than animal movement. Needless to say, when testing children, it is very important to use the correct age norms; the norms used in this book are applicable only to adults.

As we pointed out in Chapter 3, movement scores assume the presence of form. Even though the form aspect of the movement responses is practically always the dominant feature, the control implied by the different movement scores does vary. The *M* response typically implies a good amount of control; being more infantile, *FM* implies more spontaneity and less control; the *m* response points to the control being outside of the person. Consequently, to some degree one could add the consideration of movement Determinants to the above discussion on form and control.

The interpretation of the movement responses is complicated by the fact that different kinds of movement are associated with the Content of the response. In other words, the rise in the frequency of *M* is intrinsically tied to a concomitant rise in the number of human figures *(H)* that are seen on the Rorschach. As individuals mature, they are likely to report seeing more people, and more people in motion. The end result is that both of these variables *(M* and *H)* are signs of maturity and good adult functioning.

Possible Interpretations for Human Movement *(M)* Markers

Low scores (< 1, < 1): The examinee
- Is immature and childish
- Has trouble considering alternatives in problem-solving situations; associated with attention-deficit/hyperactivity disorder (Bartell & Solanto, 1995)
- Functions with a trial-and-error approach
- Is unable to delay gratification to accomplish a goal
- Is spontaneous, showing freedom to act on the spur of the moment; is less likely to think things through than to act on gut reactions and inspiration

High scores (> 7, > 8): The examinee
- Is mature and adultlike
- Is intelligent, imaginative (Cocking, Dana, & Dana, 1969)
- Is aware and purposeful in actions
- Is able to consider alternatives in problem-solving situations
- Is able to delay gratification in the pursuit of a goal
- Is intellectualized; may be unable to act before all options are taken into consideration

---

Possible Interpretations for Animal Movement *(FM)* Markers

Low scores (< 2, < 1): The examinee
- Is unable to draw from the more primitive interests and drives
- Is unable to recognize basic emotional needs
- Is unable to use fantasy to satisfy needs
- May have low intellectual ability

High scores (> 6, > 6): The examinee
- Is immature; is likely to think and behave in ways that were more appropriate in earlier years
- Displays interest and thinking more likely to be related to basic needs (except it was not found to be a valid indicator of pressing primary needs in Mihura et al.'s, 2013, meta-analysis)
- Is spontaneous; does not use much reflection or deliberation
- Is likely to use fantasy to fulfill needs
- Is unable to delay gratification in order to reach goals

People differ a great deal in their assessment of the elements of life they can master and the elements that are beyond their control. Some people feel that they can control most important aspects of their lives; others have less of this sense of mastery. Moreover, some people are optimistic about their chances of encountering fewer uncontrollable events or being less affected by the uncontrollable events (e.g., an earthquake is unlikely to happen, but when it does, my house is not likely to suffer). In summary, some individuals have a sense of invulnerability, whereas others have a sense of doom.

The elements that are beyond human control are invariably the ones that make people anxious and distressed. On the Rorschach, these elements are represented by inanimate movement, the *m* response. The blowing wind, the moving flames of a fire, and the explosion are common Rorschach responses that speak of forces that cannot be controlled. Although having a few of these associations is common, having a large number of such responses suggests that the person is experiencing life as unpredictable and unmanageable. The *m* variable is a sign of distress.

Possible Interpretations for Inanimate Movement *(m)* Markers

Low scores: Not interpretable

High scores (> 3, > 3): The examinee
- Experiences forces that are beyond his or her control
- Sees the world as threatening and unpredictable
- Experiences frustration, tension, and stress, as well as anxiety and hostility (Greenwald, 1990)
- Has a sense of impotence and helplessness; seen with self-mutilating adolescents (Kochinski, Smith, Baity, & Hilsenroth, 2008)
- Experiences disorganization resulting from a sense of being overwhelmed

Active or Passive Movement

Hamlet's dilemma, also posed by the well-known Serenity Prayer, is well expressed by his famous monologue:

> To be, or not to be, that is the question: whether 'tis nobler in the mind to suffer the slings and arrows of outrageous fortune, or to take arms against a sea of troubles, and by opposing end them. (Shakespeare, *Hamlet*, Act III, Scene I)

This is a dilemma that everyone in a problematic situation faces. As Millon (1990) noted, taking action appeals to some personality types, whereas other personality types favor the passive mode. This aspect of one's nature is also related to the sense of mastery, or the concern for uncontrollable external events discussed in the preceding section. In addition to personality tendencies, emotional states also lead to different inclinations in terms of taking action or accepting a situation in a passive manner: People who are depressed are often more inclined to be passive. In spite of how much theoretical sense the active–passive distinction makes, the research findings have not been impressive. A meta-analysis of the Rorschach indicated that the active to passive ratio *(a:p)* has little or no support (Mihura et al., 2013). We discourage the use of this measure, and it is not coded in the Basic Rorschach system.

Possible Interpretations for Active *(a)* Markers

Low scores (< 2, < 1): The examinee
- Is likely to respond to any situation through inaction, even when taking action would be more appropriate and effective
- Looks to the outside world to gratify personal needs
- Feels helpless

High scores (> 9, > 9): The examinee
- Is likely to respond to any situation through action, even when the action may be ineffective or inappropriate
- Has an exaggerated sense of mastery

Possible Interpretations for Passive *(p)* Markers

Low scores: Not interpretable

High scores (> 6, > 6): The examinee
- Is likely to respond to any situation through inaction, even when taking action would be more appropriate and effective
- Looks to the outside world to gratify personal needs
- Feels helpless

Chromatic Color

On January 15, 2009, a U.S. Airways plane with 150 people aboard ran into a flock of geese and lost both engines. Captain Chesley Sullenburger and his crew successfully landed the disabled plane on the Hudson River with no loss of life (see "Airplane Crash-Lands," 2009; this event has been fictionalized in the movie *Sully* [Eastwood, Marshall, Stewart, Moore, & Eastwood, 2016]). The audio interchange with the airport control tower at LaGuardia can be heard on the web. As one listens, one can hear tension in Captain Sully's voice, as he says "we can't do it" to the suggestion that he land at the Teterboro Airport in New Jersey. What is amazing to us as psychologists is not his skill as a pilot but the control he has over his emotions: This is a man whose emotions are not going to dictate his behavior at this pivotal time in his life. In contrast, we have almost daily examples of people (e.g., basketball coach Bobby Knight, baseball pitcher Carlos Zambrana, unwarranted Chicago police officer shootings) whose lack of control over emotions leads to maladjusted behaviors or even tragedies. (You can listen to a web recording of Bobby Knight's vulgar tirade when addressing his Indiana basketball team after a loss.) Often these were people facing a much less dire situation than Captain Sully faced, and yet there was much more of a meltdown.

Color is known to evoke affective states. The extent to which the person attends to the form of the inkblot is of great importance with color *(C)* responses. Attention to form indicates that the person is guided by boundaries and implies a certain amount of control. Consider, for instance, alternative responses to an emotionally charged situation, such as a traffic accident. The controlled *FC* response characterizes the person who acts in a reasoned and orderly manner (e.g., first doing anything necessary to prevent further accidents, then checking on the well-being of the people involved, calling for help if necessary, giving and receiving pertinent information, and so on). While responding in this manner, the person may be very aware of his or her disappointment, sadness, anxiety, or anger (the color), but these emotions are controlled, and the behavior is mostly dictated by reason.

In contrast, the emotions are more predominant in the less controlled *CF* response: The individual is likely to focus on his or her experience, thinking or complaining about the situation, focusing perhaps on the person who is blamed for the accident, while still controlling emotions to some degree. Finally, there is the completely emotional response that has no form or control, characterized by the *C* Rorschach score: The person comes out of the car yelling at the individual thought to be at fault, or starts crying or shaking hysterically, and so on. The implication of pure color *(C)* as an indicator of behavioral dyscontrol was not supported by Mihura et al.'s (2013) meta-analysis, but the lack of support may be attributable, at least in part, to the fact that out-of-control people and highly emotional situations are hard to capture.

There is something to be said for uncontrolled responses; an excessive amount of control is not always psychologically healthy. The ideal is a balance between control and the expression of a drive. A party may not be much of a party without some loosening of emotional controls and inhibitions, a loosening that allows people to act in a more spontaneous manner; Halloween is more fun if one wears a silly costume. In many subcultures, recreational drugs are used to help lower inhibitions. In contrast, emotional dyscontrol is inevitably disruptive. Even at a party, complete dyscontrol can lead to tragic events such as fights or driving under the influence. The perfect party, in Rorschach parlance, has a reasonable amount of *CF* but not much pure *C*.

Now consider a clinical case, the Rorschach of Sirhan Sirhan, the man who murdered Senator Robert Kennedy in 1968. Nearly all of his stimulated affect on the Rorschach was undercontrolled or out of control (*FC: CF + C* = 2: 7, pure *C* = 4). When aroused, he lost the ability to think or behave conventionally (e.g., nonviolently), especially when confronting a person he delusionally blamed for his brother's death (Meloy, 1992).

Training has a strong influence on the control people exert over their behavior. The training of a clinical psychologist includes how to respond calmly and rationally to emotionally charged situations in a psychiatric ward, in the office, or on the phone. Social norms also govern behavioral controls and the expression of emotion. What may be considered controlled behavior *(FC)* in one culture may be seen as loosely controlled *(CF)* or uncontrolled *(C)* behavior in another culture. The obscenities and gestures that are commonly expressed in the stands of a soccer stadium in Spain could result in an arrest for disorderly conduct in Chicago. Because people are largely a product of their culture, these differences do lead to different personality features and the need to be sensitive to cultural norms. But there is also the temperament of the individual to be considered, and that is what we can examine with the Rorschach.

Color naming *(Cn)* responses—when the individual is so attracted by the color that the Rorschach task is completely disregarded—are practically never seen; when they do occur, they are almost always an indication of severe pathology. This type of response is mostly seen with individuals whose thought processes are disorganized and dysfunctional.

Possible Interpretations for Form-Dominated Color *(FC)* Markers

Low scores (< 1, < 1): The examinee
- Either does not respond emotionally or responds without enough control

High scores (> 4, > 3): The examinee
- Is able to experience the emotion but responds in a controlled manner to the excitement
- Is able to think and plan in order to respond effectively in an emotionally laden situation

---

Possible Interpretations for Color-Dominated Form *(CF)* Markers

Low scores (< 1, < 1): The examinee
- Either does not respond emotionally or responds in a very controlled manner

High scores (> 3, > 4): The examinee
- Is driven by the emotion to the extent that the behavior is not very effective
- Tends to be carried away by the drama to the extent that the cognitive controls play a secondary role
- Displays impulsive or aggressive behavior (e.g., Gardner, 1951; Lamounier & de Villemor-Amaral, 2006; Miller, 1999)

Possible Interpretations for Color *(C)* Markers

Low scores: Not interpretable

High scores (> 1, > 2): The examinee
- Tends toward impulsive and labile discharge of emotions with no regard for appropriateness
- Is likely to have intense emotions
- May experience emotional disturbance

Achromatic Color

Because black is a color, some people may use the blackness of the inkblots in their responses while giving an appropriate number of color responses. For those individuals, the achromatic color responses *(C′)* can be seen as an extension of their use of color and should be interpreted as part of their emotional response to the environment. When chromatic color responses are not present, however, the use of *black* suggests a toned-down response to color—in other words, an individual who can respond emotionally only in a watered-down manner. It should be clear from a cursory look at funeral homes that the color black is associated with sadness and morbidity. Because of their relatively low frequency, all of the achromatic responses are typically added together into one variable: $SumC′ = FC′ + C′F + C′$.

Possible Interpretations for Achromatic Color *(SumC′)* Markers

Low scores: Not interpretable

High scores (> 3, > 3): The examinee
- Has a gloomy attitude, negative affect
- Is pessimistic

Texture

Texture *(T)* responses most typically consist of furry animal skins or fluffy clouds. Such responses imply unfulfilled affectional needs. Most protocols have only one *T* response (usually on Card VI). There are some data to show that individuals with one texture response have more secure attachments than people with higher scores (*SumT*; Cassella, 1999).

Possible Interpretations for Texture *(SumT)* Markers

Low scores (–, –): The examinee
- Is psychologically disinterested in or detached from others (Huprich, 2006)

As a group, the more severe psychopathic juveniles have a lower number of texture responses (Egozi-Profeta, 1999; Gacono & Meloy, 1991; Loving & Russell, 2000; Weber, Meloy, & Gacono, 1992).

High scores (> 1, > 2): The examinee
- Desires to be touched or to be physically close to others
- Experiences loneliness, depression
- Is oversensitive to rejection in interpersonal relationships; exhibits neuroticism (Greenwald, 1999), borderline traits (Fowler, Brunnschweiler, Swales, & Brock, 2005)
- Has affectional needs that may cloud judgment and create a vulnerability to manipulation from others; related to priests' sexual preference for adolescent boys (Gerard-Sharp, 2000)

Vista

Vista *(V)* responses involve looking at an object from afar, usually with an aerial perspective, and suggest a tendency to distance oneself from events or persons in everyday life. Vista responses occur infrequently, and the *VF* and *V* responses are found in less than 1% of protocols (Exner, 2003). Consequently, these responses are typically aggregated *(SumV)*.

Possible Interpretations for Vista *(SumV)* Markers

Low scores: Not interpretable

High scores (> 1, > 2): The examinee
- Tends to distance self from life situations
- Experiences feelings of inferiority, neuroticism (Greenwald, 1999)
- Experiences anxiety, emotional pain; engages in painful ruminative introspection that emphasizes the negative aspects of the self (Trenerry & Pantle, 1990)
- Tends to be self-critical and experience guilt
- Shows suicide risk (Exner & Wylie, 1977; Silberg & Armstrong, 1992)

Form Dimension

Exner (2003) proposed that the Form Dimension *(FD)* score was a measure of introspective capacity. This response nearly always was found on Card IV. Exner's interpretation was found to have little to no support in the comprehensive meta-analysis (Mihura et al., 2013). We discourage the use of this measure.

Possible Interpretations for Form Dimension *(FD)* Markers

Low scores: Not interpretable

High scores (> 2, > 2): The examinee
- Is likely to ruminate
- Possibly has dissociative tendencies (Brand, Armstrong, Loewenstein, & McNary, 2009)

Shading

Shading *(Y)* responses represent a tendency to focus on inconsistencies of the environment. These responses are typically associated with anxiety and the feeling of helplessness. Because of the low prevalence and the lack of interpretive distinction between *FY, YF,* and *Y,* they are typically aggregated *(SumY)*.

Possible Interpretations for Shading *(SumY)* Markers

Low scores: Not interpretable

High scores (> 3, > 3): The examinee
- Experiences anxiety, neuroticism (Greenwald, 1999)
- Shows painful affect; feels overwhelmed by life problems (Mesirow, 1999; Mulder, 1997; Small, Teagno, Madero, Gross, & Ebert, 1982; Weber et al., 1992)
- Experiences stressful situations (Blackall, 1995)
- Displays depressive resignation to life events, feelings of helplessness, passivity

---

Reflections

In Greek mythology, Narcissus saw his reflection in a pool of water and fell in love with himself. Unable to quit looking at his own image, he perished. With the Rorschach, people who give an excessive number of reflection responses are thought to have a similar problem: Their self-esteem is too high.

The story of Narcissus notwithstanding, we have trouble seeing a direct link between an inflated self-esteem and a tendency to see reflections on the Rorschach. The literature on this subject includes many studies that did not support the validity of these markers, or of the egocentricity index that Exner created with them (e.g., Loving & Russell, 2000). Moreover, reflection *(Fr, rF)* responses seem to be related to the orientation of the inkblot so that such responses are most often obtained with the card rotated 90° to the landscape position (Horn, Meyer, & Mihura, 2009). In their review of this literature, Nezworski and Wood (1995) concluded that these variables are unrelated to self-focus or self-esteem. We recommend against using this marker.

Possible Interpretations for Reflection *(Fr, rF)* Markers

Low scores: Not interpretable

High scores (> 2, > 1): The examinee
- May display narcissism, but we recommend against this interpretation

---

FORM QUALITY

Arguably the most important element of the Rorschach is the Form Quality *(FQ)*, a score that offers an indication of the effectiveness of the person's thinking and contact with reality. Before we consider specific interpretations for the ordinary *(o)*, unusual *(u)*, and minus *(–) FQ* scores, several issues should be taken into consideration. The Rorschach may be the best tool available for examining the thinking process of an individual (Kleiger, 1999). Perhaps the most dramatic and helpful protocols are those that clearly demonstrate a thought process disturbance. Two facts should be kept in mind:

- A *delusion* is a false belief. But, to some extent, whether a belief is false is left for others to decide, and it may be a matter of opinion. If the authors of this book believed that Hermann Rorschach had appeared to us, commissioned us to be his representative, and instructed us how to put together the Basic Rorschach, many may not believe us. If we truly believed that to be the case, some might think we had flipped our lid and were delusional. And yet, there is Lourdes, and Fátima, and Guadalupe, and El Cobre, instances of similar apparitions and beliefs. What's the difference? The difference is that the stories of Lourdes, Fátima, Guadalupe, and El Cobre are accepted by a segment of the population. And in our case, no one will believe the Hermann Rorschach apparition. Cervantes tells us that Don Quixote read too many books on chivalry and that the reading affected his mind. Maybe people would recommend that we stop reading Rorschach papers. The point is that an individual may be delusional and not have a thought disorder. A person may hold an erroneous and irrational conviction while maintaining a thought process that is logical, sequential, and free of oddities. In that case, looking at the thinking process through the Rorschach may not be revealing. Determining whether the individual is delusional is a matter of judgment and is not effectively done with the Rorschach.

- Many people who have a thought disorder are not psychotic. Even with the nonpsychiatric population, almost everyone has some Rorschach responses of poor quality. A thought disturbance is possible, even expected, with a variety of psychiatric disorders (e.g., Caplan, Guthrie, Tang, Nuechterlein, & Asarnow, 2001; Lee, Kim, & Kwon, 2005; Osher & Bersudsky, 2007; Peterson & Horowitz, 1990; van der Gaag, Caplan, van Engeland, Loman, & Buitelaar, 2005; Vanem, Krog, & Hartmann, 2008). Moreover, some people who have a thought disturbance do not have any psychiatric disorder. Nevertheless, identifying a thought disturbance is very helpful, even if it does not have a direct diagnostic link. When the Rorschach shows that the person has trouble thinking logically, or that the person's mentation is disorganized, the test is actually revealing a great deal about the person's functioning and how effective she or he is in daily life. A person who mixes boundaries, contaminating one perception with another (e.g., the wing of one animal becomes the head of another in the same response), does the same in everyday life, combining two different positions on an issue at the same time. The inability to think in a clear and logical manner is an obvious detriment to the person's capacity to function. As Boston slugger Ted Williams would have it, "If you don't think too good, don't think too much."

Especially with a response of poor *FQ*, we are able to gain insights with the Follow-Up Phase inquiry. Take, for instance, the response "This is Donald Trump with Hillary Clinton on his back" given to Card V. Imagine five different explanations a person might give to inquiries (the clinician's responses to the examinee are in parentheses):

1. [laughing] "Oh, I was just goofing off. I thought I would throw a wrench into the works and see what you would do."
2. "Well, now, I don't know where I saw them." (If you had to explain now how you came up with that idea, what would you say?) "I don't know what I was thinking of; I made a mistake. It doesn't look like that now."
3. "Here is Trump with his hair and Clinton right behind him." [The examinee is using the outline on the sloping side of what is typically seen as the wing of the bat on this card. Upon further inquiry, the examinee points to the profile of a face in the middle part of that slope.] (Please help me to see this the way you were thinking about it. As you were pointing to it, I see the profile of one face, but how did that lead you to think of Trump and Clinton?) "I thought that looked like Trump and then the person behind him must be Clinton."
4. "Well, that's all we hear about in the news, so I just thought of it on this card." (OK, but were you actually seeing those two people in this card?) "I don't know. Maybe these cards have something to do with the news . . ." (What do you mean?) "Everything is rigged and interconnected . . ." [Examinee continues with a non-sequitur string of ideas that are completely ineffective in explaining the perception.]
5. "No, I didn't say anything like that." (That's what I have down as your response.) "I don't know where you got that from; I didn't say it."

Explanation 1 shows a sense of humor. The response also suggests a certain antagonism or tendency not to play by the rules, and perhaps a histrionic attention-getting inclination. However, we would not see the response as indicating poor reality contact.

Explanation 2 suggests an impulsive individual who can occasionally voice terrible ideas but who is also capable of retrenching and correcting mistakes.

Explanation 3 starts with an accurate perception of what is a small part of the outline of the inkblot. That perception is inaccurately pegged as looking like Trump when it does not, and is then expanded to include Clinton. Here we have a situation in which the original response is spoiled by the enlargements. In real life, this type of individual may start with the recognition of a basic fact but then expand the perception, jumping to inaccurate perceptions and conclusions.

Explanation 4 shows an inability to focus on the task of examining the inkblots altogether. Here thoughts about what is happening on the daily news intrude to the extent that the person is unable to pay attention to the shape of the inkblot and is not aware that the free association given had nothing to do with the task at hand. In real life, this person may come up with ideas that are irrelevant and have little insight. When further pushed, this individual's functioning decompensates into possibly delusional thinking.

Explanation 5 shows either a cognitive disability (memory problems) or pathological denial. In the latter case, the individual may be inclined not to take responsibility for past actions when difficulties arise.

These are just some of the ways in which a person may respond to an inquiry after a poor or unclear Rorschach response. In most cases, obtaining a good-quality popular response (e.g., a bat for Card V) may be less revealing than following up and obtaining clarification of a questionable response.

Possible Interpretations for Ordinary (o) Markers

Low scores (< 6, < 3): The examinee
- Perceives the world in an unusual manner
- Has perceptions that are not always consistent with reality
- Is unique but at the expense of being able to function in a conventional world
- May have cognitive dysfunction, schizophrenia, other form of thought disorder

High scores (> 18, > 22): The examinee
- Perceives the world in a realistic and well-grounded manner
- May be hypernormal, inflexible, rigid, overly conventional
- In being very conventional, sacrifices creativity and individuality

---

Possible Interpretations for Unusual (u) Markers

Low scores: Not interpretable

High scores (> 12, > 9): The examinee
- Tends to be individualistic
- May exhibit disregard for convention and social expectations (seen more often with sexually offending clergy; Ryan, Baerwald, & McGlone, 2008)
- May have frequent conflicts with others as a result of an unconventional nature

---

Possible Interpretations for Minus (–) Markers

Low scores: Not interpretable

High scores (> 9, > 10): The examinee
- Displays a substantial distortion of reality, enough to have a significant impairment in functioning

High scores are possibly indicative of schizophrenia, depression, or other forms of psychopathology.

DUPLICATION

In our mind, the perception of a pair, designated *(2)*, is very similar in nature and meaning to the reflections discussed above. All the Rorschach inkblots are nearly symmetrical, and most responses involving a detail on one side of the inkblot (e.g., the blue crab on Card X) include the same perception on the other side. An adequate inquiry when the double perception is not spontaneously mentioned would most likely reveal that the person is seeing the same perception on the other side. However, we have the same issue with the interpretation of pairs that we discussed with reflections above: We don't think it tells us much about the examinee.

Possible Interpretation for Pairs *(2)* Markers

Low scores (< 5, –): The examinee
- May display lack of self-focus, but we recommend against this interpretation

High scores (> 13, > 13): The examinee
- May display narcissism, but we recommend against this interpretation

---

CONVENTIONALITY

A person's behavior is somewhat dictated by the situation he or she is facing. A wedding calls for dressing in a particular way, sitting on the appropriate side of the aisle, refraining from yelling and shouting, and so on. A person's behavior in other situations (e.g., a baseball game, a rock music concert) is much less contrived. Nevertheless, regardless of the situation, we see people who behave in unexpected ways. At graduations, there may be someone who does something unusual: One person may walk across the stage wearing huge clown shoes, another may have pinned a sign to her gown.

Unconventional behavior may be creative, as with people who think outside the box, or may be just unusual and attention seeking without indicating much talent. Nevertheless, these are people who tend to think in a way that is different. By looking at responses that are commonly obtained on the Rorschach, clinicians are able to examine how conventional the person may be. Popular scores *(P)* measure Conventionality in perception and likely overt social behavior.

Possible Interpretations for Popular *(P)* Markers

Low scores (< 5, < 3): The examinee
- Is eccentric; may not have a good sense of what most people would do in certain situations
- Has trouble seeing the world as others see it
- Is nonconformist

- Is creative; avoids the common and ordinary
- May experience maladjustment; seen with individuals with schizophrenia, obsessive–compulsive disorder, schizotypal personalities
- Is inclined to make an effort to be different
- May have mental deficiency

Low scores are seen more commonly in adolescents, children with a nonverbal learning disability, and elderly people approaching death as they lose interest in their environment.

High scores (> 8, > 8): The examinee
- Is conventional and overconforming
- Is nonrebellious; knows the expected behavior and feels a need to comply
- Is not inclined to take actions that show great independence or original thinking
- Is banal, stereotyped
- Is concerned about receiving approval from others, guarded
- Is inclined to economize and give only what is needed to complete the task
- Makes an effort to hide personally revealing information

CONTENT

The Content of the response may appear to be the most important part of the response to the layperson. To the Rorschach clinician, the Content is just one of the many elements of the Rorschach.

Content is interpreted in a more qualitative manner than other variables. Prominent in the book by Phillips and Smith (1953) are interpretations for the symbolic meaning of different Contents. They contended, for example, that five major aspects of the personality could be deduced from specific animal Contents. Although we recognize the difference between the nature of a lion and a bunny, the Phillips and Smith approach was severely criticized even by clinicians who used the Rorschach in an idiographic manner. Schafer (1954), for instance, objected to Phillip and Smith's fixed significance of the meaning of different Contents.

Some literature, however, addressed Content interpretations in a more conservative and judicious manner (e.g., Aronow & Reznikoff, 1976; Mindess, 1970; Schafer, 1954). These authors recommended avoiding inaccurate interpretations by emphasizing interpretations based on

- unique and original content, rather than a perception that is commonly associated with a particular card;
- highly elaborated responses relative to the other responses on the protocol;
- responses that show significant emotionality, in either the content itself or the way the response is given;
- remarks clarifying the meaning of the response;
- recurrent contents or themes; and
- consistency with historical data or findings from other instruments.

As noted in Chapter 3, there are many Content categories. The interpretive meaning of most of the categories is unclear. This chapter focuses on the two most prevalent categories: the human and animal contents.

The number of human responses to the Rorschach inkblots increases until the age of 10 and then remains stable through the life span (Ames, Métraux, Rodell, & Walker, 1973, 1974). All adults are expected to give human responses. When these are not obtained, it is almost imperative to investigate the finding further, possibly with the Follow-Up Phase procedures, in order to interpret the protocol correctly. The whole human, *H*, is the best of the possible human responses in that it typically demands an integration of different parts of the inkblot. A reasonable number of *H* responses suggests that the person thinks about other people with reasonable frequency.

In contrast to the other categories seen in the protocol, all Content categories, including human and animal responses, are typically examined in the context of the whole profile rather than interpreted individually. For instance, a protocol with two fictional human perceptions, *H*, and two perceptions of human parts, *Hd*, would be seen very differently if there also were three full humans responses, *H*, than if there were no *H* responses at all. If all the human perceptions in a protocol were fictional, we would think that the individual needs distance from other people and may have trouble relating.

Because of that consideration, we are handling this section a bit differently from the other sections in this chapter and will discuss the Content categories further in Chapter 5. For the purposes of this chapter, it may suffice to say that human perceptions suggest good cognitive development and an interest in interpersonal relationships (Draguns, Haley, & Phillips, 1967). Animal perceptions, common in all ages but particularly in childhood, suggest immaturity when they are too pronounced. Part and fictional perceptions, when too dominant, have the implication of a person who needs to maintain a certain distance from the world. The cutoffs given in Table 4.1 are based on the data from our unpublished meta-analyses.

ORGANIZATIONAL ACTIVITY

The Z score has to be taken from a table provided in Exner (2003). The Z score frequency, or *Zf*, is the number of times that a Z response occurred in the record and is based on the Location of the response when the parts are meaningfully integrated. As noted in Chapter 3, we have reservations about this variable. We sometimes find it difficult to decide when segments of the inkblot identified as separate objects are *meaningfully* integrated into a response and merit, as a result, a Z score. Moreover, in most cases we are not sure what the Organizational Activity scores say about the examinee. Little literature on this variable is available. As a result of these considerations, we do not recommend using this measure. Because we do not use it, we will borrow the cutoffs from Exner (2003; low < 8, high > 16) and the international norms (Meyer et al., 2007; low < 6, high > 19).

TABLE 4.1

Recommended Cutoffs for the Different Content Categories Based on Data From Our Unpublished Meta-Analyses

Code	Community Low	Community High	Psychiatric Low	Psychiatric High
H	<1	>5		>5
(H)		>3		>3
Hd		>4		>5
(Hd)		>2		>2
Hx		>2		>1
A	<4	>12	<3	>13
(A)		>1		>2
Ad	<1	>5		>5
(Ad)		>1	<1	>1
An		>3		>3
Art		>3		>3
Ay		>2	<1	>1
Bl		>1		>1
Bt		>4		>3
Cg		>4		>4
Cl	<1	>1		>1
Ex		>1	<1	1
Fi		>2		>1
Fd		>1		>1
Ge		>1		>1
Hh		>2		>3
Ls		>2		>2
Na		>2		>2
Sc		>3		>1
Sx		>2		>3
Xy		>1		>1

Note. H = Whole human; (H) = Imaginary or fictional whole human; Hd = Human detail or incomplete human figure; (Hd) = Imaginary or fictional human detail; Hx = Human experience such as emotion; A = Whole animal; (A) = Imaginary or fictional whole animal; Ad = Animal detail or incomplete animal form; (Ad) = Imaginary or fictional animal detail; An = Anatomy; internal body parts not visible from outside; Art = Objects of art such as paintings or decorative objects; Ay = Anthropology; objects with historical or cultural import; Bl = Blood; Bt = Botany or plants; skip if nature (Na) is scored; Cg = Clothing; Cl = Clouds; Ex = Explosion; Fi = Fire; Fd = Food; Ge = Geography, such as a map; Hh = Household object; Ob = Object; includes any human-made object except clothing (Cg); Ls = Landscape; skip if nature (Na) is scored; Na = Nature; Sc = Science; Sx = Sexual organs or activity or sexy clothing; Xy = X-ray.

Possible Interpretations for Z Score Frequency *(Zf)* Markers

Low scores (< 7): The examinee
■ Expends little effort in processing information
■ May have limited cognitive ability, depression

High scores (> 17): The examinee
■ Makes much effort in achieving goals and has a high level of intellectual striving
■ Has high drive and initiative

PRESENTATION

Form Quality, as noted above, is an important marker of a thought disorder. There are other disturbances of the thinking process, captured by Presentation, that impede good functioning and that do not involve perceptual inaccuracies. An examinee who saw a butterfly with five testicles on Card II was seeing the usual butterfly at the bottom of the card and had an explanation for the small bumps that are typically disregarded by others. In terms of perceptual accuracy, this response is at least as good as if not better than the usual butterfly response. However, the explanation of the small details in bizarre sexual terms suggests some tendencies that may be present in the person's thinking. The Special Scores or Cognitive Codes are used to flag those instances of faulty or idiosyncratic reasoning and classify them so clinicians can describe the kind of life problem the person may demonstrate in his or her daily life.

With the exception of two thematic codes (Cooperative Movement *[COP]* and Mutuality of Autonomy—Health *[MAH]*), Special Scores or Cognitive Codes indicate an idiosyncratic, disturbed, or illogical thought process and suggest poor functioning or confusion. If we exclude the Level 1 Special Scores (i.e., showing little or no pathology), the expectation is that a well-functioning individual would not have more than one Special Score in the protocol. Table 4.2 lists the Special Scores and Cognitive Codes and their possible interpretations.

ROTATIONS

We tested an adolescent whose parents complained that he contradicted everything they said and disregarded all of the house rules, at times for little gain. When we gave him the first card of the Rorschach, he held it from the top and, with a flip of the wrist, immediately turned it upside-down. Although he eventually gave responses with the card in the upright position, most of his responses were given with the cards upside down. Like the use of the white space, rotations can be a sign of independence or indicative of an oppositional attitude. An excessive number of rotations can be interpreted in a manner that is very similar to the excessive use of white space. Turning a card sideways increases the probability of a reflection response (Horn et al., 2009). Consequently, the card turns have to be taken into account when interpreting a high count of reflection responses.

TABLE 4.2

Possible Interpretations for Special Scores or Cognitive Codes

Code	Name	Possible interpretations
ABS	Abstract Representation	May have amorphous and unclear thought processes, trouble reasoning in a clear and stepwise fashion
		May be guided by emotions (check color responses) to the extent that the thought process is too intuitive and does not have enough logic
AG	Aggressive Content	Is likely to view interpersonal interactions as marked by competition or aggression (Mihura, Nathan-Montano, & Alperin, 2003)
AGM		May engage in interactions with others that are at least competitive and forceful, if not aggressive and hostile
AGC		May be identifying with the aggressive action or images, or may be fearful of external dangers
ALOG	Alogic or Peculiar Logic	May display illogical reasoning
PEC		May be more likely to experience illogical thinking when emotions are involved (check color responses)
CP	Color Projection	Denies irritating or unpleasant emotions
		Has difficulty dealing with negative feelings
		Tends to distort reality in order to deal with negative feelings
		Lacks insight
CON	Contamination	Is likely to mix different concepts together in a pathological manner
		May demonstrate trouble with boundaries and an inability to differentiate and keep separate different ideas or attributes
DV	Deviant Verbalization	Does not communicate effectively with others
		May appear odd because of some of the words or expressions used
		Is egocentric; functions with the apparent belief that others can almost read his or her mind (and know what is meant) even when it is not said
DR	Deviant Response	Experiences mentation problems; has difficulty staying on task when doing a job; is likely to become involved with issues that are extraneous to the task
		Has trouble maintaining adequate ideational control
		May experience unfiltered, scattered, and disjointed thinking
		May have trouble with impulse control
FAB	Fabulized Combination	Is likely to show a disregard for reality in daily life
		May experience serious distortions in thinking
		May demonstrate impaired judgment because of poor reality testing

TABLE 4.2 (*Continued*)

Possible Interpretations for Special Scores or Cognitive Codes

Code	Name	Possible interpretations
INC	Incongruous Combination	Likely demonstrates bizarre and strained logic
		May have a preoccupation that seriously interferes with thought processes
MAP	Mutuality of Autonomy–Pathology	May fear being negatively influenced or controlled by external forces
MOR	Morbid Content	Feels damaged, inferior, or unwanted; associated with obesity (Elfhag, Barkeling, Carlsson, Lindgren, & Rössner, 2004) and self-mutilating adolescents (Kochinski, Smith, Baity, & Hilsenroth, 2008)
		Is likely to emphasize negative features about the self
		May have depression (Petrosky, 2005)
		May see the environment as hostile, dangerous, or damaging and may have aggressive tendencies (Baity & Hilsenroth, 2002)
		Is concerned or preoccupied with negative occurrences such as illness or death
		May have a history of adversities or setbacks, interpersonal difficulties (Schneider, Huprich, & Fuller, 2008).
		Holds a pessimistic view of the self and the future
		May express enjoyment indicating an identification with the aggressor
ODL	Oral Dependent Language	May have feelings of inadequacy
		Feels dependent on others to make ends meet
PER	Personal Knowledge	May be in need of self-assurance in life tasks
		Is likely to be egocentric in interactions with others
		May be a criminal or violent individual (C. B. Gacono, Meloy, & Heaven, 1990; Siemsen, 1999; Young, Justice, & Erdberg, 1999)
		May alienate others because of the frequency and forcefulness with which opinions are expressed
		May be grandiose, egocentric, or narcissistic
PSV	Perseveration	May have intellectual impairment
		Is preoccupied with a concept to the extent that it interferes with the ability to function
		Could be engaging in a defensive tactic to stay with one association so that other associations do not need to be given; possibly a sign of a lack of effort in performing tasks in life

---

Possible Interpretations for Rotation Markers

Low scores: Not interpretable

High scores (> 5): The examinee
- Displays flexibility, curiosity, independence
- Displays negativism, oppositional tendency, rebelliousness
- Wishes to look at the world in a way that is different from the way it is presented, which may be an asset or a liability depending on how it is used
- Has difficulty sustaining relationships because of the inclination to be contradictory, intolerant of the usual social compromises

---

REACTION TIME

Most clinicians have abandoned reaction time *(RT)* as a measure in the Rorschach. If reaction times are acquired with a stopwatch, the labor involved in acquiring and processing the data might be greater than the usefulness of the data in the majority of the cases. When the Rorschach responses are entered into our program, Hermann, the recording and processing of the reaction times is automatic, and the *RT* measure is occasionally very useful. It has been shown that reaction times have a normal distribution and a considerable range so that some examinees have a shorter reaction time than others (Choca, Van Denburg, & Mouton, 1994).

Possible Interpretations for Reaction Time *(RT)* Markers

Low scores: Not interpretable

High scores (> 25 seconds): The examinee
- Has a low energy level, psychomotor retardation, depression (Priyamvada et al., 2009), anxiety (Vijayakumaran, Ravindran, & Sahasranam, 1994)
- Has low intellectual ability; is confused about the task
- Labors obsessively, having to think carefully over all possible options
- Is guarded, distrustful; has to consider how the different options will be interpreted
- Is resistant; does not want to do the task

Closing Remarks

This chapter reviewed the possible meanings of single Rorschach markers. Interpretations at this level are similar to the interpretations of single scale elevations in a questionnaire such as the MMPI–2. Chapter 5 considers interpretations that take into account more than one Rorschach marker. Continuing with the analogy, that approach would be reminiscent of questionnaire interpretations that take into account two or three scales at the same time. Chapter 6 discusses examination of the entire protocol or profile as one entity.

Mixing and Matching Variables | 5

C hapter 4 of this volume looked at Rorschach measures in isolation, but measures are often more meaningful when considered with other measures. As we tell our students, the answer to nearly every counseling question is, "It depends." It's often that way for Rorschach interpretation too. A boy with a mental age of 6 years is highly intelligent if he is only 4 but would be considered intellectually deficient if he were 10. A person with a dependent–histrionic personality looks very different from a person with a dependent–schizoid personality. It is usually a mistake to interpret the meaning of individual markers in isolation from other Rorschach data. To interpret the Rorschach with sophistication, clinicians have to mix and match the measures covered in Chapter 4. This chapter reviews the important elements that need to be compared and contrasted; Chapter 6 examines interpretations of the entire profile.

Important Considerations for Mixing and Matching

Numerous Rorschach systems have been developed to explore important but often highly specific issues. There are systems to examine the prognosis of psychiatric patients, the extent of a formal thought disorder, the quality of

http://dx.doi.org/10.1037/0000075-006
Assessment Using the Rorschach Inkblot Test, by J. P. Choca and E. D. Rossini

object relations, the level of oral dependency, possible distortions of body image, the extent of primary process thinking, the use of defense mechanisms, and so forth (for more details, see Bornstein & Masling, 2005). We have no doubt about the usefulness of such systems in particular cases. However, for our own work, we have aimed to remain as close as possible to what the examinee was doing, and we do not favor complicated calibrations as a matter of routine.

We even discourage the use of some of the derived measures that are typically part of the Structural Summary. Consider the Adjusted *D* score in the Comprehensive System (CS), supposedly an indication of stress tolerance. This index starts with the computation of the Experience Actual *(EA)* as the sum of human movement responses and the weighted sum of the color responses. The Experience Stimulation *(es)* is then computed by adding animal and inanimate movement to achromatic color and to all shading responses. This is followed by the determination of a differential score, the Adjusted *es* score, obtained from a conversion table. This Adjusted *es* score is subtracted from the *EA* score, and the value is converted into an Adjusted *D* score through the use of another conversion table. If you are like us, by now your head is in the stratosphere, too far removed from anything you can observe the examinee doing that would be of interest. Like Kleiger (1999), we believe in the usefulness of "deconstructing the various scoring categories in order to ascertain the psychological experiences that underlie the scores" (p. xiii).

We believe Rorschach markers can be interpreted in a number of different ways for different examinees. We strive to discover what a particular marker means for a particular examinee. Even valid markers are not valid for everyone. An excellent marker in clinical psychology may be valid only 80% of the time (Baldessarini, Finklestein, & Arana, 1983). The examinee in front of us may be one of the 20% for whom a particular interpretation does not apply. B. L. Smith (1997) noted that "even the best predictors from the Structural Summary are often inaccurate in specific cases" (p. 192). We understand why clinicians have grouped Rorschach scores to examine important constructs (e.g., susceptibility to current stress). However, that approach implies that the measures being aggregated have only one correct interpretation, which is usually not the case.

Consider another example, the CS Aspirational Index. This index takes the whole inkblot *(W)* score to be a measure of the person's aspiration, and human movement *(M)* to be a measure of psychological resources. Those assumptions may be viable for a number of examinees. However, many other interpretations of the *W* and *M* markers are possible (see Chapter 4). If the clinician discovers that the *W* or *M* marker for a particular individual was driven by some other element besides aspiration and resources, then the entire rationale for the Aspirational Index becomes untenable.

Besides the Aspirational Index, there are many other ratios and composites that we will leave out of our discussion. Those composites, and the literature available about them, have been reviewed elsewhere (e.g., Choca, 2013; Exner, 2003; Meyer, Viglione, Mihura, Erard, & Erdberg, 2011; Rose, Kaser-Boyd, & Maloney, 2001). Below, we review the mixes and comparisons that we take into consideration.

Interpreting Composite Measures and Ratios

Just as in Chapter 4, we offer possible interpretations for low and high scores, but this time for combined measures rather than individual ones. We also review potential interpretations for different ratios, such as what it means when one measure is greater than, less than, or equal to another measure. In the text boxes below that look at low and high scores, the first cutoff in parentheses is derived from our unpublished meta-analysis of the community samples, whereas the second comes from our unpublished psychiatric meta-analysis; both were derived using 1.5 standard deviations from the mean. In cases where the low cutoff (mean of the meta-analysis minus 1.5 standard deviations) was close to zero, we don't provide a cutoff value (e.g., the low cutoff for unusual detail, *Dd*); in such cases, we advise the reader that a low score is uninterpretable. N/A (not available) is used when no information was available from a meta-analysis. Some text boxes feature ratios instead of low and high scores.

PRODUCTIVITY

When examining a long protocol, clinicians have to keep in mind the impact that the high number of responses *(R)* has on other measures. In terms of Location, for instance, there are a finite number of responses that can be effectively given using the whole inkblot. Unless the protocol includes many responses of poor quality or perseverative repetitions, the high *R* protocol will have many large detail codes *(D)* and small detail codes *(Dd* or *d)*. The number of different Determinants may also be high, as may the number of Content categories.

LOCATION

The number of *Dd* or *D* responses will rise with the use of white space *(S)* because many white space responses are coded as details. The use of white space should be considered in conjunction with the number of popular responses. There is also an inverse relationship between *S* and the Form Quality level of all responses *(FQX)*, suggesting that both of these measures are related to Conventionality (Traenkle, 2002). The portion of minus Form Quality responses that use white space is referred to as the *S*–% variable. A high *S*–% marker suggests that distortions of reality more likely result from anger and negativism.

**Possible Interpretations for Minus Form Quality Responses
Using White Space *(S–%)* Markers**

Low scores (–): Not interpretable

High scores (> 2, > 2): The examinee
▪ Becomes disorganized; is likely to distort reality in situations evoking an oppositional attitude

---

DETERMINANTS

Looking at the Location bar graph we presented in Figure 4.1, we again note that the higher the form or shape *(F)* bar is, the lower the Determinant frequencies on either side of that bar are going to be. Graphs with lower *F* bars will show higher Determinant frequencies on one side or the other. An abundance of Determinants on the left side suggests an emphasis on internal functioning and on the right side points to a higher reactivity to external events.

Movement

A good balance between human movement *(M)* and animal movement *(FM)* is indicative of a person who is sufficiently mature to have the inner stability that allows delay of immediate gratification and sufficiently self-accepting to allow the integration of personal needs (Klopfer, Ainsworth, Klopfer, & Holt, 1954).

Possible Interpretations for Human Movement *(M)* Markers

*M > 2 * FM:* The examinee
- Is mature and adultlike
- Is intelligent, imaginative (Cocking, Dana, & Dana, 1969)
- Is aware and purposeful in actions
- Is able to consider alternatives in problem-solving situations
- Is able to delay gratification in the pursuit of a goal
- Is intellectualized; may be unable to act before all options are taken into consideration

M = FM: The examinee
- Is capable of deferring gratification without undue conflict or inhibition

*2 * M < FM:* The examinee
- Is immature; is likely to think and behave in ways that were more appropriate in earlier years
- Displays interest and thinking more likely to be related to basic needs
- Is spontaneous; does not use much reflection or deliberation
- Is likely to use fantasy to fulfill needs
- Is unable to delay gratification in order to reach goals

In terms of the active *(a)* versus passive *(p)* movement distinction, we have noted the lack of literature support. Nevertheless, the balanced ratio is thought to be two active responses for every passive response. Such balance implies that the person is able to consider both active and passive solutions. A reasonable number of movement responses (> 3) are necessary before this comparison would be meaningful.

Possible Interpretations for Active *(a)* and Passive *(p)* Movement Markers

a > **4 * *p*:** The examinee
■ Is likely to respond to any situation through action, even when the action may be ineffective or inappropriate
■ Has an exaggerated sense of mastery
■ Displays mania or narcissism

a = *p*: The examinee
■ Experiences Hamlet's dilemma: uncertainty about which option to take
■ Is ambivalent and indecisive about any action

a < *p*: The examinee
■ Is likely to respond to any situation through inaction, even when taking action would be more appropriate and effective
■ Tends toward fantasy or rumination
■ Looks to the outside world to gratify personal needs
■ Feels helpless
■ Engages in passive escape, preventing problem solving and personal initiative
■ Experiences depression

Color

To evaluate external reactivity, the color Determinants are often combined as *SumC* = *FC* + *CF* + *C*, where *FC* is a form-dominant color response, *CF* is a color-dominant form response, and *C* is a color response with no form.

Possible Interpretations for Color *(SumC)* Markers

Low scores (< 1, < 1): The examinee
■ Displays a low level of emotionality

High scores (> 8, > 5): The examinee
■ Is affectively overemotional
■ Has histrionic personality traits

In addition, it is useful to take an overall account of the kind of color responses in the protocol. The color ratio (*FC:CF* + *C*) compares the controlled color responses with those that are less controlled.

Possible Interpretations for Color *(FC, CF,* and *C)* Markers

FC > **2 * (*CF* + *C*):** The examinee
■ Is overly constricted emotionally and has little contact with emotions

---

---

2 * *FC* < *CF* + *C*: The examinee
■ Has weak control over emotions
■ Is labile and overreactive; has histrionic personality features (Blais & Hilsenroth, 1998; Blais, Hilsenroth, Castlebury, Fowler, & Baity, 2001)
■ Shows risk of impulsive responding to emotional situations or aggressive acting out (Miller, 1999; Siemsen, 1999)
■ Is likely to have poorly modulated, unrestrained, and disorganized affect
■ May have little regard for the effectiveness of the emotional response

---

The weighted color sum *(WSumC)* emphasizes problems with emotional dyscontrol if they exist. This composite groups all of the color responses together but gives more weight to the responses that reflect less control. The calculation is done as follows: *WSumC* = 0.5 * *FC* + *CF* + 1.5 * *C*.

Possible Interpretations for Weighted Color Sum *(WSumC)* Markers

Low scores (<1, <1): The examinee
■ Shows disinterest in emotionally stimulating aspects of the environment
■ Tends to respond in a muted, unemotional manner to events

Low scores have been found in examinees with Asperger syndrome, emotional problems (Holaday, Moak, & Shipley, 2001), and pain (Holaday, 1998)

High scores (> 5, > 6): The examinee
■ Displays liveliness and emotive reaction to life events

High scores have been correlated with extroversion (De Carolis & Ferracuti, 2005). High scores have been found in individuals suffering from panic disorder or agoraphobia (de Ruiter & Cohen, 1992).

Blends

Consider a discussion of an important national issue, such as immigration reform. Some argue for a simple solution that typically will not work because it leaves many factors out of consideration (e.g., all undocumented immigrants should be deported and we should not allow any more to come in). In contrast, there are those who want to consider so many aspects at the same time that the issue becomes too complex to handle effectively (e.g., the impact of immigration on the economy and crop growers; and the impact of deportation on family integrity and welfare; and the impact of immigration on international relationships; and the impact of immigration on national systems such as education, taxes, and Social Security; and the political consequence of taking a position). For many tasks, the deferral of action until all aspects are considered would result in never taking any action at all. More useful than either of these extremes is a thought process that takes enough factors into consideration to handle a portion of the problem in a reasonably adequate way, even if it is clear that some issues will remain. Effective thinking can be neither too simplistic nor too complex.

At this point we have talked about the Determinants as if there were only one Determinant per response. In actuality, however, approximately 20% of Rorschach responses are *blended*; that is, they have more than one Determinant (Exner, 2003). The number and kinds of blends that appear on a record give information about the complexity of the thought process of that individual.

A blended Determinant implies that the individual can appreciate the complexity of the inkblot and is aware that more than one aspect of the inkblot contributed to his or her thinking of a particular response. One issue associated with blends is intellectual capacity. People who are cognitively capable have more ability to recognize the aspects of the inkblot that suggested the response and to communicate those aspects to the clinician (Petot, 2005; Tibon, 2000). In reasonably intelligent individuals, the number of blends speaks to the expansiveness or narrowness of their thinking, the flexibility of their thinking, and whether they search to discover the subtleties that influenced their thinking on a response or are content with fulfilling the minimal requirement. The complexity of the response may also be a measure of the stress, needs, and conflicts experienced by the individual: The more uncomfortable people are in their lives, the higher the level of complexity shown in their thinking.

Possible Interpretations for Blend Markers

Low scores (< 1, < 1): The examinee
- Displays thinking that is too narrow
- Tends to neglect or ignore the richness and complexity of the environment
- Shows repression, constriction, guardedness
- Experiences depression (Goldman, 2001)

High scores (> 8, > 8): The examinee
- Displays overly complicated thinking and psychological operations
- Shows disorganization, confusion, and unpredictability due to overload
- Experiences mania, schizophrenia

A color–shading blend is one that has a color Determinant *(FC, CF,* or *C)* with either an achromatic color *(FC', C'F,* or *C')* or a shading (i.e., texture *[FT, TF, T]*; vista *[FV, VF, V]*; or shading *[FY, YF, Y]*) Determinant. This blend represents emotionality (the color) with signs of depression and pain (the achromatic color and shading).

Possible Interpretations for Color–Shading Blend Markers

Low scores: Not interpretable

High scores (> 1, > 1): The examinee
- Displays a thought process that is too complex as a result of anxiety and depression
- Experiences emotion as painful
- Has negative feelings that spoil positive emotions

High scores have been seen with suicidal children (Petot, 2005).

Affective Ratio

The Affective Ratio *(Afr)* is computed by dividing the number of responses on the last three cards (which are color cards) by the number of responses on the first seven cards. The *Afr* is a measure of emotional reactivity. Because the colorful cards included are the last cards, the ratio also speaks to how productive the person is after doing a task for a period of time.

Color cards are likely to produce more responses than achromatic cards (Exner, 1962; Silva, 2002). If the number of responses to all of the cards were equal, the *Afr* would be .43. However, as the number of responses given to the last three cards increases relative to the number of other cards, the ratio increases. An *Afr* of 1.0 means that the examinee spent the same amount of energy on the last three cards as on the preceding seven cards. To interpret the *Afr* marker, the clinician has to decide whether the marker was emotionally driven or driven by a changing level of comfort in dealing with the task.

Possible Interpretations for Affective Ratio *(Afr)* Markers

Low scores (< .25, < .22): The examinee
- Is not as emotionally responsive as most people
- Does not know how to vent feelings
- Mistrusts feelings and attempts to keep them under control
- Is not enthusiastic about activities in life
- Avoids and withdraws from emotionally laden material
- Does not allow the self to fully interact with the world
- Is likely to become tired and to stop working after some period with a task
- May be experiencing depression or suffering (de Ruiter & Cohen, 1992; Holaday, 1998)

High scores (> .85, > .78): The examinee
- Becomes energized when presented with emotional stimuli; may have a tendency to get caught up in emotion
- With high *F* count, seeks emotional stimulation but does not respond to it
- Is likely to be constrained at the beginning of a task but becomes more productive as comfort increases with what is expected

---

CONTENT

This section examines the combinations of Content categories and the relevant contrast between some of the categories.

The compilation of all responses with human content, *SumH*, provides a measure of interpersonal interest and awareness. The calculation is done as follows: $SumH = H + (H) + Hd + (Hd)$, where *H* is human content, *(H)* is imaginary or fictionalized human content, *Hd* is human part or detail, and *(Hd)* is imaginary or fictionalized human part or detail.

Possible Interpretations of Human Content *(SumH)* Markers

Low scores (<2, <2): The examinee
- Has limited interest in people
- Is preoccupied with the self or issues that do not involve people
- Displays social avoidance
- Has interpersonal problems

Low scores have been reported with children experiencing disruptions in caregiving and attachment (McCarroll, 1998), criminals (Walters, 1953), juvenile delinquents (Ray, 1963), and people with schizophrenia (Sherman, 1952; Vinson, 1960).

High scores (>11, >11): The examinee
- Is driven by interpersonal needs to the extent of disregarding other elements of life

---

The R-PAS combines the number of fictional or part human responses, a measure called Non-Pure-Human *(NPH)*. Thus, $NPH = (H) + Hd + (Hd)$, and a proportion is also computed as $NPH / SumH$. The cutoffs for *NPH* in the text box were taken from R-PAS data (Meyer et al., 2011).

Possible Interpretations for Non-Pure-Human *(NPH)* Markers

Low scores: Not interpretable

High scores (>6): The examinee
- Views self and others in a fanciful and unrealistic manner
- Has an active fantasy life
- Has trouble viewing others as intact, independent whole persons

H > 2 * NPH: The examinee
- Is able to see others as distinct entities
- Is able to establish and maintain interpersonal relationships
- Experiences people as a whole rather than in fictional views or fragmented parts

2 * H < NPH: The examinee
- Has an unrealistic perception of others
- Has fantasized and unrealistic expectations of interpersonal interactions
- Distances the self from others in that other people are seen only in part or as unreal figures

---

FORM QUALITY

With a typical examinee, the Form Quality of the responses is usually the same throughout the protocol. However, sometimes the quality of the responses suffers or improves as the examination progresses, and for some examinees the Form Quality may be different for the achromatic and the chromatic cards. It is sometimes useful to compare *MQ*, the Form Quality of the human movement responses, with that of the entire protocol; *MQ–* is the number of human movement responses of minus Form Quality. If there were to be a difference in quality between human movement responses and other responses, the clinician would have to determine the reason for the differential. Similar thinking leads diagnosticians to look at the Form Quality of *F* responses *(FQX–)* or responses using white space *(S–)*.

Possible Interpretations of Minus Human Movement *(MQ–)* Markers

Low scores: Not interpretable

High scores (> 2, > 2): The examinee
▪ Shows lack of clarity in the understanding of people
▪ Has disturbed interpersonal relations
▪ Maintains beliefs that interfere with the realistic appraisal of others

---

SPECIAL SCORES

The Six Special Score Sum *(Sum6)* is a compilation of the count for the six most prominent Special Scores, as follows: *Sum6 = DV + DR + INC + FAB + CON + ALOG* or *PEC*, where *DV* is Deviant Verbalization, *DR* is Deviant Response, *INC* is Incongruous Combination, *FAB* is Fabulized Combination, *CON* is Contamination, *ALOG* is Alogic, and *PEC* is Peculiar Logic. This sum is considered to be a good measure of cognitive slippage in problem solving.

Possible Interpretations for Six Special Score Sum *(Sum6)* Markers

Low scores (< 1, < 3): The examinee
▪ Displays efficient thought processing
▪ Is able to focus on a task without extraneous intrusions

High scores (> 6, > 8): The examinee
▪ May have a thought disorder
▪ Tends to have the thought process disrupted by extraneous and egocentric intrusions, even if able to see reality in an accurate manner
▪ Experiences psychosis, schizophrenia

The weighted summary of the six Special Scores *(WSum6)* consists of all of the variables of *Sum6* but weights the count by the level of the severity of the response. Thus, *WSum6 = DV1 + DV2 * 2 + INC1 * 2 + INC2 * 4 + DR1 * 3 + DR2 * 6 + FAB1 * 4 + FAB2 * 7 + PEC * 5 + CON * 7*, where 1 indicates Level 1 responses (indicating little or no pathology) and 2 indicates Level 2 responses.

Possible Interpretations for Weighted Six Special Score Sum *(WSum6)* Markers

Low scores (< 4, < 19): The examinee
▪ Displays efficient thought processing
▪ Is able to focus on a task without extraneous intrusions

High scores (> 18, > 45): The examinee
▪ May have a thought disorder
▪ Tends to have the thought process disrupted by extraneous and egocentric intrusions, even if able to see reality in an accurate manner

High scores have been found in children with learning disabilities (Brainard, 2005). High scores may be indicative of psychosis (Brand, Armstrong, Loewenstein, & McNary, 2009; Peterson & Horowitz, 1990; Vanem, Krog, & Hartmann, 2008).

Closing Remarks

In Chapter 4, we reviewed the meaning of single measures or markers. This chapter discussed the interdependency of those single markers. Chapter 6 takes an even broader view and considers interpretation approaches. The book then moves on to discuss other ways of analyzing the Rorschach experience, as well as future possibilities for the Rorschach.

Interpreting the Results
A Four-Step Framework and
Advanced Interpretation Strategies

6

B y now we have shared with you our understanding of the Rorschach (see Chapter 1), covered its administration (Chapters 2) and scoring (Chapters 3), and discussed the simple and complex measures that make up the Structural Summary (Chapters 4 and 5). Now, "the time has come," as the Walrus would have it in Lewis Carroll's (1871) poem, "to talk of many things: Of shoes—and ships—and sealing-wax—of cabbages—and kings—and why the sea is boiling hot—and whether pigs have wings . . ." (p. 27) and of Rorschach findings and what they may mean.

A Four-Step Framework for Interpreting Rorschach Scores

The job of establishing meaning spans the entire diagnostic task and includes much more than the Rorschach. But the Rorschach, in the hands of a capable diagnostician, can make a unique contribution. We next describe the four steps that we follow in harvesting Rorschach findings.

http://dx.doi.org/10.1037/0000075-007
Assessment Using the Rorschach Inkblot Test, by J. P. Choca and E. D. Rossini

STEP 1: ADMINISTRATION

Diagnostic work focuses on discovering one thing: what kind of a person the client is. By the time the administration is finished, the observant clinician should have ideas about what information can be ignored and what information should be emphasized, using both behavioral observation and a familiarity with the array of possible global patterns described below. Once clinicians have mastered efficient Rorschach administration, the task becomes mechanical, even boring, if they do not approach it with the clinician's eye. What makes administering a Rorschach interesting is an inquisitive mind constantly wondering what led the examinee to offer the response obtained.

The level of confidence clinicians have when they make a statement in their report may be related to how well they pursued their intuitions with the client during the administration. A notably poor response on Card IV, in a protocol with otherwise good responses, could have been caused by a myriad of reasons. If the clinician was able to actively follow up that poor response with prompts and questions, he or she may be more confident when asserting that the client is likely to decompensate in situations involving a powerful figure, or in situations that elicit powerful dysphoria, or in situations that evoke a need for affection. Thus, the first hypotheses clinicians put down on scratch paper in preparation for writing the report may come from the test administration process itself.

STEP 2: ITEM INTERPRETATIONS

Hellmut Brinkmann (personal communication, 2015) encourages clinicians to pay attention to the thought processes used in supporting a response. An association that started with a detail may confine itself to the original detail, or it may be expanded into a larger area when revisited. Staying with the original detail suggests that the examinee is the type of person who is likely to attend to an idea without going beyond it or getting off track. Such focus may be a very good trait to have, especially if the original idea was reasonable and if it was supported in a competent manner. A good example may be the bowtie in the center of Card III, described later as being red, having a knot in the middle, and having a loop on each side. This thought process likely indicates the kind of individual who attends to the problem at hand without being distracted by other issues.

A different thought process is revealed by a response that starts with an area and expands the Location into further areas, which may even be enlarged to include the whole inkblot. An example from Card III is a response that begins with two people, the popular response for this card. Upon further reflection, however, the individual expands the original idea to include other parts: the center bottom detail becomes a table that the two people, now seen as waiters, are setting up, and all of the red details are then seen as decorations in the party room. The inclination to elaborate a concept may have advantages and disadvantages. In this example, the initial response benefited from the expansion, growing in detail and richness, revealing the thought process of a person who likely mulls an idea over and is able to embellish it in creative ways.

But consider the person who expands the perception of the two waiters serving the table by adding two red hearts in the middle and two upside-down monkeys on the sides. If the person insists that these ideas are to be part of the same response, then a different form of elaboration, a psychopathological one, is evident. This expansion is still faithful to the card's shapes but does not make sense as an integrated whole concept. In this case, the expansion spoiled what was originally a good response, in spite of the fact that it showed good perception of the shapes. In interpreting this response, the clinician should consider the possibility that the person was so affected by the emotion evoked by the red details that the areas had to be included impulsively, without working through to a reasonable integration. Another hypothesis is that the person was driven to put everything together, even if some things did not quite fit.

The issue during the Follow-Up Phase may be how much work the clinician has to do before the examinee can concoct a vision that provides a real integration of these details or—better yet—reorganizes these perceptions as three different responses. In real life, this person may be inclined to string one idea or task to the next, without ever realizing that simple pictures are best. Perhaps a family portrait can be best accomplished by not putting the three dogs, the two cows, and the kangaroo into the picture.

Other types of spoiling expansions may be even more concerning. Take a response that starts with the alligator's head in the right bottom detail on Card V but proceeds to see the entire alligator in the rest of the inkblot. Here the expansion betrays a disturbed thought process. This is the type of thinking that may go from the accurate observation of a gentleman sitting in a black car in front of a building, to the conviction that we are under surveillance by the FBI. To sum up, there are people who expand on a concept productively and creatively, and there are people who should have quit while they had the chance. Moreover, something can be said for simplicity and against expanding every task beyond its original target.

Although we have focused on response processes that involved an expansion of the original concept, many other interesting thought processes could possibly be deduced from examining the tendencies seen during the Inquiry or Clarification Phase of administration. The clinician must pay attention, for instance, to idiosyncratic phrases, repetitive phrases, or unusual preoccupations or interests, and to the typical thought progression used in supporting the response. Borrowing a metaphor from the psychotherapy literature, Rorschachers need to "listen" with their peripheral vision.

STEP 3: THE STRUCTURAL SUMMARY

The computer program Hermann compares the client's scores with what is expected using three different normative samples (Choca, 2017). This task could also be done by hand using the values from our meta-analyses offered in Chapters 4 and 5 or by consulting the original sources. Once the clinician knows what scores are outside the expected range, he or she can jot down possible interpretations for the low and high markers. Often the clinician is able to discriminate between the possible interpretations that are likely to be valid and those that clearly do not apply to this client. For example, the hypothesis of intellectual deficiency for a low number of responses *(R)* marker is not tenable if the client is a recent college graduate with no history of neuropsychological problems.

Further examination of the Structural Summary allows the clinician to put his or her findings together. Advanced interpretive approaches, including profile analysis, are discussed below. However, before clinicians develop the expertise of taking in the entire profile and examining the Structural Summary at a macro level, they can take steps in that direction by considering some of the findings together. For instance, there is only one way to have a low *R* protocol, and that is to have everything else be low; any high marker in such a record is worthy of notice. A high *R* protocol, on the other hand, can be accomplished in a multitude of ways, and clinicians should look at other aspects of the Structural Summary to determine the manner of approach of the individual, the range of Determinants and Contents, the level of Conventionality, the Form Quality of responses, or the presence of Special Scores. An examination of a high Affective Ratio *(Afr)* can be complemented by looking at the amount of control shown by color responses. A high or low form or shape *(F)* marker calls for taking into account the other Determinants. Observations can also often be made about the range of Content categories in the protocol.

STEP 4: SEQUENCE ASSESSMENT

Finally, the clinician's interest turns to the other tendencies that he or she may be able to infer from the protocol. Looking at each card, the clinician should note differences in the way the examinee responded to the card and whether the differences reveal anything about the examinee (i.e., sequence analysis). Taking into account the entire protocol, the clinician searches for global trends. Was the approach to the test different at the beginning than at the end? For example, one can compare the very first response to Card I (signature response) with the last response on Card X (sign-off response). Which cards led to responses of low quality? Was the individual able to recover on Card V if responses of low quality were given before that card (Peterson, 2010)? Was there a difference in the handling of chromatic or achromatic cards? of structured and unstructured cards? The Rorschach is a serial problem-solving task with subsequent cards influenced by what was seen on previous cards. Some clients are exhausted by the Rorschach, whereas others are invigorated.

Again, we believe the Rorschach is at its best when used as a clinical investigative tool, not as a measuring device. The time clinicians take to score the responses and examine the Structural Summary is profitable only if it serves to highlight tendencies the client demonstrated during the session. The first part of this chapter provided a glimpse of how the Structural Summary scores could be integrated with the available observations in order to generate diagnostic insights.

Advanced Interpretation Strategies

Now that you have learned the four steps of interpretation, it is time to find out what Rorschach variables speak to you directly. You are ready for advanced interpretation strategies.

Advanced interpretation is not harder or more complex than basic interpretation, but it is individually tailored to the way you want to understand people, and geared toward the populations you assess. Advanced interpretation does not involve committing to memory all of the Rorschach psychodiagnostic hypotheses meticulously catalogued by Ogdon (2001).

Advanced interpretation answers two questions: what other Rorschach variables make the most sense clinically, and whether a global approach is useful to you. Advanced Rorschach interpretation involves one or both of two additions to your Rorschach repertoire, either at the micro or macro end of the spectrum: learning specific noncanonical constructs and learning a global model of interpretation (e.g., personality styles or psychodiagnostic patterns).

MICRO RORSCHACH CONSTRUCTS

Let's begin with some potentially interesting constructs not from the Comprehensive System (CS) or the Rorschach Performance Assessment System (R-PAS). Hundreds of Rorschach interpretive constructs have been invented over the years. Some have generated considerable clinical interest for a time, but most have dissolved, largely unused, into the fog of Rorschach history. Some represented considerable intellectual and theoretical heft (e.g., Blatt & Ford's, 1994, Concept of the Object Scale). Some have been developed in response to perceived clinical needs now considered outlandish (e.g., signs of male homosexual orientation), whereas others focused on promoting a specific personality theory.

This chapter introduces a number of constructs and structural models that you may find useful. The R-PAS has adapted several of these into its system. Three Content-based constructs are currently popular in assessment practice and research and seem to directly address the clinical questions ideally answered by the Rorschach: Extended Aggression Scores, the Oral Dependency Scale, and the Mutuality of Autonomy Scale.

Extended Aggression Scores

Anger, aggressive behavioral problems, and victimization are all-too-real issues in clinical practice, as is phobic fear of one's own aggressive impulses. Historically, the Rorschach has done a poor job in accessing these strong cognitive and affective states.

Forensic psychologist Carl Gacono and his colleagues provided a possible remedy for this weakness by developing more precise aggression-related scores to supplement the CS Aggression Content *(AG)* construct. These scores were developed because of perceived false negative limitations in the utility of the standard CS code aggressive movement *(AGM)*. In addition, the single CS *AG* score was shown to have little to no support in the recent Rorschach meta-analysis by Mihura, Meyer, Dumitrascu, and Bombel (2013).

Discussions of each extended aggression score can be found in the literature (Gacono & Evans, 2008; Gacono, Gacono, Meloy, & Baity, 2008). Two scores, Aggressive Content *(AgCon)* and Past Aggression *(AgPast)*, have reasonable psychometric support as well as clinical usefulness. Three other, less frequent scores remain more speculative at this time: Aggressive Potential *(AgPot)*, Aggressive Vulnerability *(AgVul)*, and Sadomasochism *(SM)*. *AgCon* is the most frequent extended aggression score across studies. It is coded for any content that seems dangerous or malevolent or that could cause harm (e.g., "It's a switchblade"). *AgPast* is coded for violence or aggression that has already happened (e.g., "a cat that has been run over by a truck"). It is considered to represent vulnerability to masochism or victimization or some other type of traumatic self-damaged perceptions.

Do elevations (markers) on these scores indicate that a person is aggressive? Perhaps. If a person had several *AgCon* scores, a better way to look at it would be to state, "This person is more stimulated by aggressive impulses than the typical person" or "This individual seems vulnerable to engaging in more aggressive behavior than most people." What these scores cannot do is to identify either the "villain" or the "victim" definitively in any interpersonal aggressive relationship without additional information.

Oral Dependency Scale

Psychological neediness, dependency, and related personality traits are currently popular in the literature (e.g., Bornstein, 2005). The fifth edition of the *Diagnostic and Statistical Manual of Mental Disorders (DSM;* American Psychiatric Association, 2013) retained the dependent personality disorder. The projective assessment of dependency and dependent personality traits has primarily used the Rorschach Oral Dependency *(ROD)* Scale (Masling, Rabie, & Blondheim, 1967). Bornstein and Masling (2005) succinctly noted that

> a key strength of the *ROD* scale is the simplicity of its administration, scoring, and interpretation procedures, which have remained unchanged for more than 35 years. Because these procedures are highly standardized, clinicians and researchers can obtain usable *ROD* data with minimal training. (p. 136)

To score the *ROD*, one simply counts the number of responses involving oral, food, or related content (Bornstein & Masling, 2005, Table 5.1) and divides by the number of responses in the protocol *(R)*. The *ROD* content score can be used for both categorical (High Dependency vs. Low Dependency) and dimensional interpretation. Interpretation is straightforward. The mean proportion of oral-dependent responses among nonclinical college students was .13 and among psychiatric patients, .11. Gender differences were negligible. High scores indicate heightened dependent traits, orality in the immature sense, and probable issues with interpersonal sensitivity and insecure attachment. Low scores imply low dependent needs or dependency conflicts.

Mutuality of Autonomy Scale

Urist (1977) introduced the Mutuality of Autonomy *(MOA)* scale as a content-based way to capture how people mentally perceive themselves and relationships on a 7-point developmental continuum ranging from interactive and adaptive (mutually autonomous) to pathologically destructive. The Rorschach Research Council considered adding the *MOA* to the canon but ultimately rejected its admission into the CS. The R-PAS added a modified version of the *MOA* into its canon, coding responses for the healthiest level (Level 1) and a composite psychopathological score using Levels 5, 6, and 7.

Sophisticated meta-analyses support the validity of the *MOA* in both the original and aggregated score (Graceffo, Mihura, & Meyer, 2014). Although the initial work was done to assess child psychopathology, the *MOA* is now a life-span construct. An ordinal-level score (1–7) is assigned to all relationships. The relationships can involve humans, imaginary beings, animals, or even natural environmental forces. Implied relationships, such as reflection responses, are also coded.

The following level descriptors are adapted from Urist (1977, p. 4) with our own examples of scored relationships:

- Level 1: Figures are engaged in some relationship or activity in which they are together and involved with each other in such a way that conveys a reciprocal acknowledgment of their respective individualities (e.g., two ladies playing a kettle drum together).
- Level 4: One figure is seen as the reflection or imprint of another. The described relationship conveys a sense that the definition or stability of one object necessarily requires the other because it is merely an extension or reflection of the other (e.g., Narcissus seeing his reflection in the pool).
- Level 7: Relationships are characterized by an overpowering, enveloping force. Figures are seen as swallowed up, devoured, or generally overwhelmed by a force completely beyond their control (e.g., the creature in the movie *Alien* that is sucking the life out of the astronauts [G. Carroll, Giler, Hill, & Scott, 1979]).

Graceffo, Mihura, and Meyer (2014) noted that "many different well-reasoned summary scores exist for the *[MOA]*" (p. 582). Interpretation requires selecting from among the scoring options. Many clinicians follow Blatt and Ford's (1994) suggestion to simply compare the person's highest and lowest *MOA* scores, using these as bookends of the person's capacity for healthy interpersonal relating and their most pathological vulnerability, with the mean *MOA* score being the average expectable way of relating. The R-PAS has an adapted *MOA* construct.

MACRO STYLES AND GLOBAL PATTERNS

Astronomers estimate that approximately 6,000 stars are visible from North America with the naked eye. Among these stars, 88 distinct star patterns, called *constellations*, have been identified, most since antiquity (e.g., Big Dipper, Orion's Belt). Although meaningless in themselves, these constellations immediately identify specific regions of space. They rapidly orient us to where we are looking within the vastness of space. Humans seem programmed to seek out patterns and commonalities from disparate information. So, too, with Rorschach behavior: Clear patterns emerge. The Rorschach is a problem-solving task, and understanding the big picture of how a person typically responds to complex problems is an essential aspect of clinical assessment. There is a long history of attempts to define types of Rorschach responders. For example, the original starting point for interpretation in the CS was called the Four Square (Exner, 1974). Beginning with the Experience Balance (*Erlebnistypus*), three traitlike patterns or coping styles were identified: extratensive, introversive, and ambitensive. These distinctions never seemed useful in clinical practice, except perhaps in the extreme variants.

Clinical Prototype Matching

The earliest approach to clinical prototype matching began with Hermann Rorschach himself. Schafer (1948) described in encyclopedic detail the prototypical Rorschach profiles for 12 groups of pre-*DSM* psychiatric patients (e.g., Obsessive–Compulsive Neurosis, Narcissistic Character Disorder) and five subgroups of patients with schizophrenia. His attempt was to identify common prototypes that suggested each type of psychopathology, a diagnostic pattern-matching model of interpretation. This was a popular diagnostic strategy for many years from the postwar era until the emergence of the CS (see, e.g., Rapaport, Gill, & Schafer, 1968).

Rorschach clinicians asked the question, Which clinical group does this client's protocol most resemble? That became the starting point to render a specific diagnosis. For example, in attempting to define one pathognomonic pattern, Schafer (1954) noted that "the experience balance *(EB)* is the principle indicator of the hysterical neurosis in the Rorschach Test. With very few exceptions, sum C exceeds M and M is 1 or 0" (p. 35). An early version of the CS presented specific norms for several clinical groups, and pattern-matching diagnostic inferences were common.

These clinical norms were ultimately discontinued, although some clinicians continue to seek patterns. For example, in the definitive book on Rorschach assessment of personality disorder, nine of the 12 presented cases have a Structural Summary texture Determinant score of $T = 0$ (Huprich, 2006). This should make sense for people with personality disorders, as they have problems with conventional close interpersonal relationships and the conventional acknowledgment of intimacy needs. Is $T = 0$ a pathognomonic sign of personality disorder? No, but it is an interesting, experience near indication of the significant interpersonal limitations expected among people with characterological psychopathology.

In a less disturbed sample, Harrower and Bowers (1987) identified seven discrete profile types from an otherwise highly homogeneous group: doctoral students in clinical psychology studying the Rorschach (e.g., the Very High R, the High $F\%$, the High M, and the Introvert). Even within a nonclinical population, clear Rorschach patterns emerged and predicted some important aspects of the students' behavior.

More recently, Choca (2013) identified eight clinical patterns, largely independent of *DSM* diagnosis, detectable among inpatient and outpatient populations: Guarded Minimal Compliance, Cognitive Impairment, Overcontrolled Micro View, Rebellious Antagonism, Impulsive Overemotional, Thought Disorder, Morbid Dysphoria, and Hyperenergized Euphoria. His book provides extended discussions as well as diagnostic and treatment implications for each profile; brief introductions follow.

Guarded Minimal Compliance

The Guarded Minimal Compliance profile is characterized by relatively few responses, superficiality, and lack of embellishment among neurologically intact clients. This profile usually has only *F* Determinants, and the Content is the obvious. Passive–aggressive inferences are usually made in these cases. In real life, these people seem to be merely going through the motions without authentic personal commitment or engagement across life tasks. However, this pattern is modal among clients with significant intellectual limitations without the passive–aggressive inference.

Cognitive Impairment

Although often similar to the Guarded Minimal Compliance profile, the Cognitive Impairment profile is typically found among neuropsychological populations. In fact, clinicians of previous generations were probably introduced to the (then) emerging field of clinical neuropsychology through Z. Piotrowski's (1937) 10 Rorschach signs of organicity. The similarities between this profile and the Guarded Minimal Compliance profile include few responses and unelaborated, superficial responses. However, the Cognitive Impairment profile usually includes confusion, perseverative responses, and even Special Scores or Cognitive Codes.

Overcontrolled Micro View

Like the previous profiles, the Overcontrolled Micro View profile is constricted, but in a markedly obsessive–compulsive manner. This profile has an average or greater than average number of responses, but small details are focused on, and Determinants tend toward *F* and some movement and shading. Clients may seem as if they are trying to be precise, correct, and meticulous. Because their perceptual abilities are constricted, so too are their affective states and creativity. The Rorschach is hard work for these people, and they often check in to see if they are doing what is expected.

Rebellious Antagonism

The Rebellious Antagonism profile is usually preceded by hostile or critical comments about the testing, the examiner, or the inkblots themselves. Card rotations, white space responses, and aggressive content are common. Some clients, especially rebellious adolescents, provide exaggerated sexual responses both to shock the examiner and to express their superiority. Attributions of dyssocial, antisocial, and oppositional traits are obvious.

Impulsive Overemotional

The Impulsive Overemotional profile is characterized by impulsivity (i.e., rapid reaction times) and responses that have to be amended during the evaluation. Whole responses and common details are seen, and undercontrolled chromatic color is often prominent.

These people often try to add numerous additional responses during the Inquiry or Clarification Phase. Youth with attention-deficit/hyperactivity disorder are often found to have this profile, as are adults with impulsive traits. These people leap before they look.

Thought Disorder

The Rorschach has a long history in the assessment of thought disorder and milder cognitive slippage (J. F. Murray, 1992). Some consider this to be the most unique and valuable aspect of assessment that the Rorschach provides. The Thought Disorder profile manifests a high number of Special Scores, inaccurate visual perception (poor Form Quality), interpersonal ineptness, and insufficient control over affective and impulsive forces. Poor boundaries are another attribute, usually in the form of combinatory thinking, such as conflating one response into another.

Morbid Dysphoria

The Morbid Dysphoria profile is often constricted (High $F\%$ or High Lambda) but fraught with considerable, painful emotion, revealed by a large number of achromatic color responses and shading responses paired with morbid content. Using the Extended Aggression scores is useful in this case. Some clinicians consider the psychoanalytic diagnosis of *hysteroid dysphoria* for clients who are markedly depressed and in acute dysphoric pain. We teach our students to mentally translate the word *dysphoria* to *misery* to fully understand the pain of the person before us. Because empathy can get in the way, it is difficult to take the Rorschach of a person manifesting a Morbid Dysphoria profile.

Hyperenergized Euphoria

The Hyperenergized Euphoria profile is the converse of the Morbid Dysphoria profile. These people give many (often, too many) responses in an animated, effortless, even jovial manner. Many fantasy-creative and affective dimensions are evident (movement, chromatic color), as are card rotations and white space responses. Our students refer to these clients as being "on a caffeine high," suggesting hyperactivity, hypomania, and related states.

Levels of Personality Organization

Finally, in deference to the psychodynamic history of the Rorschach, we introduce a contemporary (and pragmatic) analytic approach—seeing a global level of personality organization pattern—based on the developmental model of Otto Kernberg. This approach was expanded into a Rorschach assessment textbook including many annotated cases for each of the three levels, Neurotic, Borderline, and Psychotic (Meloy, Acklin, Gacono, Murray, & Peterson, 1997). Among the various psychodynamic constructs available, Kernberg (1984) paid close attention to three indices reflecting distinct developmental lines: identity integration, defensive operations, and reality-testing capacity. Using Rorschach scores, Acklin (1992, 1993, 1994) has described in detail the characteristics of each level of personality organization. This approach answers an important question: How disturbed is this client, all things considered? Because our respect for our colleague Marvin Acklin is second to none, we rely on his descriptions of the Neurotic, Borderline, and Psychotic protocols in this section.

Neurotic Protocols

The control of anxiety and developmental conflicts define neurosis. "The typical neurotic Rorschach demonstrates notable ego-limiting mechanisms—constriction, conventionality, and inhibition of drive-laden material" (Acklin, 1994, p. 6). Additionally, "one might expect the neurotic record to be characterized by banality (high Populars, high Intellectualization Index) without elevation of validity indicators (Lambda), affective overcontrol, . . . generally adequate reality testing, . . . and immaturity" (p. 7).

Borderline Protocols

People with borderline personality organization and borderline personality disorder manifest fundamental psychological deficits. Broadly speaking, one would anticipate a protocol that reflects ego weakness, general instability of psychic functioning, and easily provoked regression. The borderline Rorschach is typically, but not always, raw in content, in both affective and content spheres; it also offers a mixture of human percepts ranging from cooperative to malevolent (Acklin, 1993, p. 337).

Psychotic Protocols

Rorschach protocols organized at the acutely psychotic level are unmistakable. The psychopathology jumps out at the clinician across domains. Acklin (1992) noted that, among other cognitive and object relations deficits, one

> might expect to find the following Rorschach characteristics: loading up of Special Scores, especially Level 2 special scores; a heavily Weighted *Sum6*; . . . disturbances and oddities of syntax and representation indicative of thought disorder; . . . deterioration of Form level; . . . disturbances in the structural features of percepts, . . . especially human percepts; . . . failure of defensive operations and utilization of primitive defenses. (p. 460)

Concluding Remarks

Our four-step model of interpretation prepares you to interpret the Rorschach with confidence. Advanced interpretation allows you the freedom to select from among the hundreds of Rorschach constructs developed over the years, choosing those that best help you understand the uniqueness of your client.

Finding the Person Behind the Scores

7

enry A. Murray (1938), the theorist who also codeveloped the Thematic Apperception Test (TAT; H. A. Murray, 1943), coined the term *personology* as the psychological study of the whole person. We think of Rorschach clinicians as personologists. We also agree with the conclusion Vaillant (1977) reached after his longitudinal research on accomplished men's lives: People are simply "too human for science, too beautiful for numbers, too sad for diagnosis, and too immortal for bound journals" (p. 11). It's time to resurrect the person as the real focus of the assessment, to look through the scores at the examinee in front of us.

We mentioned in Chapter 1 that the introduction of the Rorschach in the United States was marked by the rivalry between Bruno Klopfer and Samuel Beck. A charismatic and engaging individual, Klopfer was a gifted clinician with the uncanny ability to cut through an individual's facade and dig into the important issues. Klopfer had a scoring system (Klopfer, Ainsworth, Klopfer, & Holt, 1954), but he was mostly interested in the interaction with the examinee. Beck (1950), in contrast, was a serious empirical scientist. For him, the Rorschach provided the ability to compare the examinee with a group; the uniqueness of the individual was portrayed as the single element in the ocean of individual differences. When both of these pioneers died, the Exner era began.

http://dx.doi.org/10.1037/0000075-008
Assessment Using the Rorschach Inkblot Test, by J. P. Choca and E. D. Rossini

In the 1970s, John Exner dedicated himself to the integration of the various Rorschach scoring systems. The multiplicity of systems had been a bit like the Tower of Babel and had made communication among Rorschach experts difficult. Exner succeeded in taking the best others had to offer and formulating the Comprehensive System (Exner, 1974), a system that soon became the standard throughout the world.

Although he aimed to integrate the different approaches to the test as well, he did not do so. Exner had the heart of an empiricist. He was much more in tune with Samuel Beck than with Bruno Klopfer. The Exner era left us in the United States with journals that publish only empirical studies. This is most ironic in the case of the *Journal of Personality Assessment*, the journal Klopfer founded in 1936 as the *Rorschach Research Exchange*. Although some U.S. practitioners during the Exner era persisted with the clinical approach (e.g., Aronow & Reznikoff, 1976; Aronow, Reznikoff, & Moreland, 1994), most had to visit South America or Europe, and read publications like *Rorschachiana*, to find the Rorschach clinician.

With Exner's death, two camps established themselves in the United States, as noted in Chapter 1. Both of these camps emphasize the science. One has to go outside the United States to hear clinical presentations and seminars. Perhaps it's time to reclaim the Rorschach from what we call the *empiricist's pawnshop*, which refers to psychologists who insist on a rigid, empirical approach that we feel undermines the Rorschach's clinical richness and impedes creative administration (Choca, 2015). As can be seen throughout the present book, we are not wishing to abandon the science or the scoring. But we are wanting to bring back Bruno Klopfer and put the clinician back into the U.S. Rorschach world.

The purpose of psychological testing is to work on behalf of the client in front of us. As clinicians, we have a fiduciary relationship with our clients. We work *with* the referring professional, but *for* the client. The tests themselves, and their multiple scores, are simply tools or means to that end. Learning such a complex and cumbersome test as the Rorschach, beginners often lose sight of the person being evaluated.

There are four traditions in psychology: empiricism, rationalism, materialism, and romanticism (King, Viney, & Woody, 2013). Empiricism, stressing numbers, is mostly *nomothetic*—learning about an individual by comparing the person with a group. The other three traditions are more *idiographic*—wanting to understand the person as a unique entity. *Rationalism* focuses on reasoning as its primary methodology. The focus on humans' biological makeup is found in the tradition of *materialism*. Finally, *romanticism* seeks to find the essence of being that is missing in other approaches. The Rorschach empirical effort has led to impressive achievements, and we dedicated much of Chapters 3 through 6 to cover the empirical approach. But the stress on the empirical, nomothetic effort has also limited the utility of the instrument.

Much of the psychoanalytic work exemplifies the rational tradition. Psychoanalytic approaches continue to have some hold over assessment psychologists to use projective tests (e.g., Bram & Peebles, 2014). The classic psychoanalytic Rorschach literature (e.g., the work of David Rapaport and Roy Schafer) was based on drive theory. The idea is that innate id drives are often in conflict with the ego and the superego. The intensity of the affect associated with that conflict can lead to a flooding experience that overwhelms the individual.

More recent psychoanalytic work includes ego psychology, object relations, and self psychology. Ego psychologists can use the Rorschach to examine ego strength and the person's ability to tolerate anxiety. The issue of whether an individual can see others as entities in their own right or can see people only egocentrically, in the way those people affect the individual, is part of the object relations approach. The examination of boundaries between Rorschach responses may shed light into the person's ability to distinguish different entities. The person who mixes in the alligator head with the wing of the bat on Card V may have similar boundary differentiation difficulties when it comes to human beings. Finally, the Rorschach may be used to examine the person's affective control and the awareness the person has about his or her emotional reactions, the interest of self psychology. Information about control can be gathered from the Structural Summary, and the awareness is a question that can be pursued in the Follow-Up Phase. The problem with these approaches is that they may be too advanced or philosophical for most readers to comprehend, accept, or make productive use of (e.g., the book on self psychology by Silverstein, 2007).

At a less theoretical level, a rational approach can be used to integrate the individual's history and interview information with the test data. For instance, oppositional Rorschach markers (e.g., card rotations, reversal of the figure–ground perspective) can gain in importance when the presenting complaint of an adolescent examinee is negativistic behavior at home. In that case, what may have been unimpressive empirical markers can gain weight because they are supported by rational evidence.

Moreover, our Follow-Up Phase typically relies on a rationalism-based methodology. For instance, a college woman who was the victim of date rape had difficulty producing a response on Card VI. In the Follow-Up Phase, we learned of her awareness of and discomfort with the sexual aspects of that card. This is a case in which the empirical Structural Summary may have shown no sexual responses and may not have been very revealing. Here, our interest in pursuing the person, in seeking what was behind the examinee's difficulty in producing a response, was more productive than the empirical evidence.

The Rorschach is not part of the usual neuropsychological battery because we have better instruments to measure cognitive functions. However, attending to the tradition of materialism may occasionally pay off. There are patients who do not have neuropsychological complaints but whose Rorschach protocols show confusion and some of the other signs that Perry and colleagues highlighted in their work with cognitively impaired people (Perry & Potterat, 1997; Perry, Potterat, Auslander, Kaplan, & Jeste, 1996). We remember a man who kept insisting the inkblots were actual pictures, distorted by us to make the objects more difficult to see, even after being told several times what the pictures were. He turned out to be in the early stages of a dementing illness. In some cases, the person we find hiding behind the inkblots is not the person we expected to see.

Finally, clinicians should keep in mind the much-forgotten tradition of romanticism. The Rorschach may not be very helpful in detecting an existential crisis over a loss of meaning in life, but we have found the romantic tradition useful in pointing out the positives. Much too often, the diagnostic work focuses on problems and limitations, but there are also strengths in every protocol. There is a real human being who may have a sense of humor, a creative bent, a wish to please, or a wish to put a foot down and show uniqueness by not going along with our expectations, a real human being who may want to impress us with Productivity and give more responses than we may want, or who may be too shy to give us the number of responses we think we need. What we are after is that real human being. To find that human being, we can start with the numbers of the Structural Summary, but we must be willing to go beyond those numbers.

Ideally, psychological testing is an open-ended, question-answering endeavor. The real referral question is to discover, Who is this person? or, stated differently, What kind of person is this? At both levels, the focus returns to the uniqueness of the person being evaluated.

Consider literary examples. Beck's (1976) unusual book *The Rorschach Test Exemplified in Classics of Drama and Fiction* used actual Structural Summary codes and Rorschach scores to describe the behavior and moment-to-moment psychological struggles of such fictional characters as Hedda Gabler and King Lear. The codes were used to define personality issues, conflicts, and behavior changes in these dramatic characters' lives. But the focus of the book was on the immortal fictional people themselves. The Rorschach scores were used to demonstrate the invisible process or the forces operating on or within that person. In another example, Leichtman (2004) reminded us that Tennessee Williams's most famous character was administered the Rorschach in a scene rarely performed on stage (Gussow & Holditch, 2000). The fading, but acutely traumatized, Southern belle's response to Card V was as follows:

> It's a butterfly, a fragile and exquisite creature that once roamed free, but now, is caught in the net of a naturalist. It will be pinned down and studied with a cold eye by a man who has no sense that it was once a living, breathing, vibrant being. (as quoted in Leichtman, 2004, p. 306)

Leichtman's interpretation splendidly refocuses us on her and not her "response," noting that "the quality of the elaboration, notably the attribution of characteristics such as delicacy, sensitivity, and refinement, suggest that the response incorporates qualities she wishes to ascribe to herself and, in fact, seems to be enacting as she gives it" (p. 306). It is impossible not to feel empathy for her, or to see her psychological essence based on this response.

Translation Into English From CS-Speak or R-PAS–Speak

The final product of clinicians' work is the psychological report. Often this report is read by people who know very little about the Rorschach, and perhaps not much about psychology in general. For these reports to be useful, the findings have to be explained in plain and easy language, in a manner that can be understood by people outside the profession. As an example, Choca (2013) noted that the statement "The Rorschach protocol had many responses where color was used in an uncontrolled manner" is meaningful only to those who are well versed in the use of the Rorschach. A better statement of the same information would be, "The Rorschach indicates that Mr. Smith is likely to be carried away by his emotions in emotionally charged situations, to be impulsive, and not to be thoughtful and controlled enough" (Choca, 2013, p. 209). For a client with texture score of $T = 3$ (High Dependency), the report could state, "Mr. Johnson is needy, and significant others probably find him clingy and annoying to be around." For a client whose weighted sum of the six Special Scores is $WSum6 = 56$, indicating thought disorder, the report might state, "Ms. Jones speaks in ways that nearly all others find peculiar, even 'crazy.' People probably avoid interacting with her because of the odd, even bizarre, way she communicates."

Now consider a longer Rorschach interpretation that focuses on the person but uses the Rorschach scores as evidence of the interpretation. Yalof (2006) provided a case study of a child, Allen, with suspected Asperger syndrome and a possible nonverbal learning disorder:

> On the Rorschach, Allen was responsive beyond age expectations *(R)*, hyperfocused on details that others might quickly ignore *(Dd)*, and not attuned to the more common or conventional aspects of his environment (Populars, *D* Locations; *Xu%*). He was also formal in his response style (Lambda), confused (*PTI; WSum6; FD*– in blend with content suggestive of loss of distance/perspective), and in a state of cognitive overload (*Zd; m; D* score) that appeared to border on obsessive thinking. . . . These characteristics appeared to support my experience of Allen as having problems with self-monitoring; responding in ways that were uncommon; asking me questions that others would not consider raising; and interacting in an overly formal, somewhat pedantic, but affectively powerful (*M:C* ratio) manner even if occasionally out of sync *(CF; Ma–)* with my sense of the emotional tone of our interaction. (p. 26)

Closing Remarks

This chapter emphasized the importance of finding the person hiding behind the data collected. Sometimes a clear sense of who the client is emerges easily as you proceed with the diagnostic process. At times, there is a Rorschach marker, a response, a TAT story, a self-report test profile, or something else, that offers a portrait of the individual with uncanny clarity, sort of like the painting of a face that almost shows what the person is thinking.

On many other occasions, however, you have to work at it. In those cases, it may be useful to commit to memory as much of the data as possible and let it sit. Go for a walk, go swimming, take a long shower, have a seat in your thinking armchair, and do whatever you do when your brain is likely to produce one of your great insights. If you succeed, you are ready to write, and you should go on to read Chapter 8.

Sometimes, unfortunately, the muse eludes even great clinicians, and you'll end up having to write up a case without a comfortable breakthrough conceptualization. Those are the limitations you have to accept as long as you have made the effort, as long as you are not just running patients through an assembly line. The Rorschach is not a good assembly line instrument.

Writing Effective Reports
Show and Tell

8

Writing a psychological test report puts closure on the Rorschach assessment experience. Report writing is often given little attention in training courses. This is so in spite of the fact that the test report is the part of this work that most people see and hence should merit much attention. Moreover, perhaps as a result of poor training, many psychological reports are unfortunately written in a way that makes them hard to read, not particularly informative, and boring. We recommend that our students read fictional literature that describes personalities well (e.g., Chekhov's [1892/1993] "Ward No. 6," Thurber's [1942] "The Catbird Seat," Goncharov's [1859/1915] *Oblomov*, Roth's [1959] "Defender of the Faith," Mann's [1898/1936] "Tobias Mindernickel"). We encourage readers to pay attention to how the author accomplished the characterization of the protagonist. We have found ways to make the learning of report writing less arduous and more rewarding. Several skills are needed: the skill of extracting the important information, the skill of translating into English the books' CS-speak or R-PAS-speak, the skill of integrating data from other sources, and the skill of organizing the report. In this chapter, we develop these ideas and present a full case report.[1]

[1]Additional full case reports are available online at http://pubs.apa.org/books/supp/choca.

http://dx.doi.org/10.1037/0000075-009
Assessment Using the Rorschach Inkblot Test, by J. P. Choca and E. D. Rossini
Copyright © 2018 by the American Psychological Association. All rights reserved.

Extracting the Important Information

Ideally, psychological testing is an open-ended, question-answering endeavor. The data gathered during the execution of a typical full battery are much too extensive to be included in a report. Consequently, the writer has to decide what information is important and what information can be set aside. Assessment questions come from three sources: the referring clinician, the client, and the test data. Most importantly, the referral questions need to be directly answered, or the report needs to explain why the questions cannot be answered. Later, any and all questions that the client poses directly need to be answered (e.g., Why does this inpatient hospitalization keep happening to me?). Finally, questions that emerged from the assessment process itself need to be addressed.

Regardless of the referral questions, we believe there is also a universal, though unspoken, referral question the writer needs to keep in mind: Can I say something important about this person that is not already known? To accomplish that well, the writer needs to have a coherent conceptualization of who the examinee is (see Chapter 7). That conceptualization then needs to be organized and explained in the report. That conceptualization, and the scheme used to explain it (see below), should also guide the writer's decision as to what information should be included and what information can be set aside.

Translating Rorschachese Into English

A good report is one that Homer Simpson could read and understand. The following is an example of a somewhat technical, two-paragraph Rorschach interpretation, one part of a longer report for Leo, an early adolescent with superior intelligence and considerable visual–perceptual talent who was prone to aggressive verbal outbursts exclusively within the family system:

> Leo's fewer-than-average Rorschach responses were brief and unelaborated, but the content was conventional and age appropriate. There were no indications of impaired perception, significant cognitive slippage, or underlying thought disorder. There were no indications of vulnerability leading toward eruptions of borderline-like psychopathology. However, his problem solving was a fairly literal, childlike "it-is-what-it-is" style, with little elaboration or engagement with his inferred emotional or creative personality resources. The emotions that were stimulated tended to be age-appropriate anxiety appearing on the more unstructured and provocative Rorschach cards.
>
> Adaptively, Leo revealed himself to be capable of affective control, even overcontrol, as well as to be conventionally person-related under ideal conditions. Less adaptively, he seems quite conflicted. To achieve this level of internal control, he needs to shut down his considerable emotional and creative–imaginative personality resources. His Rorschach profile was more anxious than depressive, but again in a defensively overcontrolled manner. In older terminology, Leo's personality development seemed to be blocked and organized at the "neurotic" level.

Competent as that writeup clearly is, note the difference when the same data are communicated in a more person-focused and readable manner:

> Leo can present himself as a fairly typical adolescent, except when strong feelings are experienced. He then shuts down and acts like a simpler and quite immature child, prone to throwing tantrums. His thinking and worldview are reasonably normal, and he is not a severely disturbed youth by any means. Rather, he is a quite conflicted guy actively trying to keep control over his feelings and impulses at the expense of his psychological growth. His verbal aggression seems to be an acting out of these conflicts, reducing internal pressure in a way that is self-esteem enhancing. What you see as oppositional behavior he experiences as "macho" behavior; being a "man not a mouse." The overwhelmed, frightened, and anxious self-image has to be hidden from all significant others, whatever the expense. If he could not throw a tantrum to blow off steam, Leo would likely become quite depressed.

Integrating Data From Other Sources

The Rorschach is not used as a stand-alone instrument. It is usually part of a larger, multimodal testing battery that includes historical information from a variety of sources and personality inventories. In current times, with the emphasis on time management needs, many clinicians make frequent use of self-report questionnaires, instruments that obtain information from the examinee while consuming relatively little time from the examiner. One has to keep in mind that many of these instruments are self-presentation measures and may present an intentionally or unintentionally biased view, but in the best of cases, a wealth of good information can be derived from such tools. Several books or book chapters (e.g., Choca, 2004, 2013; Ganellen, 1996; Kvaal, Choca, Groth-Marnat, & Davis, 2011), as well as a spate of journal articles (e.g., Finn, 1996), discuss integrating Rorschach findings with other tests.

New students sometimes write test reports that are actually a regurgitation of the presenting complaints and the client's history. That information should have been covered in the history part of the report and does not need to be duplicated in the test report section. Nevertheless, there may be important details of the presenting complaints or the history that can be further explained with the test results or used to support the test findings. In that case, the writer can briefly remind the reader of the information in the test results section.

Each questionnaire used in the battery may have findings that are very revealing of our client. Again, not everything that is learned from the questionnaires may need to find a place in the report, but this information may be productively used to complement the findings of the projectives. For example, the projectives are often not that useful in diagnosing a disorder from the *Diagnostic and Statistical Manual of Mental Disorders* (fifth ed.; American Psychiatric Association, 2013), such as depression, for which the Minnesota Multiphasic Personality Inventory—2 (Butcher, Dahlstrom, Graham, Tellegen, & Kaemmer, 1989) or the Personality Assessment Inventory (Morey, 1991) may be better, or in delineating a personality style, for which the reader may use one of the Millon inventories (e.g., Millon Clinical Multiaxial Inventory—IV; Millon, 2016).

Organizing the Report

How do you develop a Rorschach writing scheme? This skill may be the hardest to develop, but it is the one that—together with the case conceptualization—has the most creative potential for the writer. The organization of the report is also a skill developed in a very personal manner. Georgia O'Keefe never signed her paintings; when asked about it, her response was something to the effect that her signature was actually all over the painting. Some of us would like to think we have developed enough of a personal style that someone could read a report and decide whether or not it was our work.

However, there are several schemes for organizing assessment data (for more information, see Choca, 2013). From our point of view, the least sophisticated scheme is to share the findings with a test-by-test progression. A more developed version of the same scheme is to group similar instruments together. With such a scheme, the Rorschach findings typically lead to one or two paragraphs in the "Personality Assessment" section of a report. One could use a caption such as "Projective Inference" as a heading for that section. Perhaps the most common organizational scheme maps report by psychological functions. A section labeled "Intellectual Assessment" may be followed by "Personality Style and Organization," followed by "Emotional Assessment," and so on.

Finally, the most sophisticated scheme is one that finds a theme for the particular examinee, a theme that tells his or her story in a way that is totally unique, interesting, and revealing. Even experienced experts, however, cannot achieve that level of creativity every time they write a report.

Case Example

At this point, we can put everything together by looking at an actual case. The client was a 16-year-old female inpatient hospitalized following a suicide attempt (information has been changed to protect the confidentiality of the individual). She cut her abdomen on Father's Day, seemingly in reaction to her father's death 3 years earlier. Major points from the Rorschach are as follows: Her reality-testing capacity was intact and conventional; there were no indications of serious cognitive slippage or formal thought disorder; her interpersonal relatedness was conventional and adaptive; and her emotional sensitivity and reactivity were quite labile compared with peers. In addition, while trying to be defensive and strong, intellectualized anger or resentment emerged; this anger or resentment fueled her depression and dysphoria (e.g., anger turned inward). Exhibit 8.1 reproduces this client's evaluation report.

EXHIBIT 8.1

Evaluation Report of a Suicidal Adolescent

```
                              -- H E R M A N N 8 --
Rorschach Protocol                                                    Page  1
================================================================================

1:     Card I                           Reaction Time: 0.00
       SCORE=>W o F O A P
       a butterfly
       INQUIRY: the big wings
       looks like there is an insect in the mid
       ANYTHING ELSE? no
       INSECT IN MID? well, like the body of the butterfly

2:     Card I                           Reaction Time: 7.80
       SCORE=>W o F O A PSV
       a fly, an insect of some sort
       INQUIRY: is big here and it has some claws
       ANYTHING ELSE? these are the 2 eyes
       ANYTHING ELSE? no

3:     Card I                           Reaction Time: 11.26
       SCORE=>D o F - Ge  >
       > a continent
       INQUIRY: this looks like Africa here, Europe here and Asia here
       ANYTHING ELSE? these little dots are like islands
       ANYTHING ELSE? this little dot looks like a sea
       ANYTHING ELSE? no

4:     Card II                          Reaction Time: 2.25
       SCORE=>W o FC O A 4.5
       a crab
       INQUIRY: these 2 look like the claws sticking out in front and the red
       ANYTHING ELSE? the general shape
       ANYTHING ELSE? no

5:     Card II                          Reaction Time: 13.13
       SCORE=>DS o F O A
       the inside part looks like a stingray
       INQUIRY: just the shape of it
       ANYTHING ELSE? the tail a
       ANYTHING ELSE? no

6:     Card III                         Reaction Time: 3.35
       SCORE=>D o Ma O (2) H.Hh P
       2 people talking to each other
       doing some work of some sort
       INQUIRY: they are leaning over and talking to each other because they are looking
       at each other
       ANYTHING ELSE? that must be the work down there
       ANYTHING ELSE? no

7:     Card IV                          Reaction Time: 12.42
       SCORE=>W o mp.FD O (H) P 2.0
       looks like one of those robo cops that changes into something else
       INQUIRY: the huge feet, the arms, that looks like a long nose and 2 eyes
       ANYTHING ELSE? it looks so big, it goes back, like it's looking down at u
       ANYTHING ELSE? no
```

(continues)

EXHIBIT 8.1 (Continued)

Evaluation Report of a Suicidal Adolescent

```
                                -- H E R M A N N 8 --
Rorschach Protocol                                                    Page  2
================================================================================
  8:     Card IV                          Reaction Time: 4.78
         SCORE=>W o F O (A) 2.0 PSV
         a large lizard
         INQUIRY: the narrow nose, funny arms, the tail. The big legs, it looks like
         Godzilla
         ANYTHING ELSE? No
         FOLLOW-UP: HERE YOU FIRST SAID A LARGE LIZARD AND THEN YOU CALLED IT GODZILLA, ARE
         THOSE TWO THE SAME? No. I thought it over and I think Godzilla fits better

  9:     Card V                           Reaction Time: 2.69
         SCORE=>W o F O A P 1.0 v
         another butterfly
         INQUIRY: v the wings & the antennas
         ANYTHING ELSE? no, the shape

 10:     Card V                           Reaction Time: 8.02
         SCORE=>W o FC' O A 1.0  v
         v a bat
         INQUIRY: because it's dark and black. Turn it upside down (but turns
         it ^). The antennas again, the darkness.
         ANYTHING ELSE? no

 11:     Card VI                          Reaction Time: 12.58
         SCORE=>W v F u Hh  v
         v a snow flake, a fake one for decoration
         INQUIRY: ^ is connected to the ceiling, it's hanging here. The shape
         ANYTHING ELSE? no

 12:     Card VII                         Reaction Time: 25.10
         SCORE=>D o FT O (2) A  v
         v kind of looks like 2 dogs on the side
         INQUIRY: the shape, it looks fluffy. The ear, the tail, and these down here r legs
         and an eye
         ANYTHING ELSE? no

 13:     Card VIII                        Reaction Time: 11.15
         SCORE=>D o FMa O (2) A P >
         > 2 animals of some sort on the sides
         INQUIRY: look like beavers, 4 legs
         ANYTHING ELSE? it looks as if it has a face
         ANYTHING ELSE? the shape I guess. It looks like it's climbing up something
         ANYTHING ELSE? no

 14:     Card VIII                        Reaction Time: 7.41
         SCORE=>D o ma.CF u Sc.Fi
         >^ the mid looks kd of like a rocket
         INQUIRY: the nose, the body, and the fire coming out
         FIRE? it's orange
         ANYTHING ELSE? no

 15:     Card IX                          Reaction Time: 18.56
         SCORE=>D o F O Ex  v
         v looks like a picture of the bomb in Hiroshima, with the smoke on top
         INQUIRY: v the mushroom here
         ANYTHING ELSE? no
```

EXHIBIT 8.1 *(Continued)*

Evaluation Report of a Suicidal Adolescent

```
                                -- H E R M A N N 8 --
Rorschach Protocol                                                      Page  3
================================================================================
16:     Card X                          Reaction Time: 11.37
        SCORE=>D o F O Hd
        looks like a long narrow face in the mid
        INQUIRY: hair, 2 eyes, the nose, a little goatee
        ANYTHING ELSE? no

17:     Card X                          Reaction Time: 10.87
        SCORE=>D o FC O Cg.(H) 1.0 PSV.AB
        like a king or something, with all the stuff around him
        INQUIRY: that's the face for the king, that wd b like his cloak, all the colors of
        royalty and prosperity
        ANYTHING ELSE? no
```

(continues)

EXHIBIT 8.1 (*Continued*)

Evaluation Report of a Suicidal Adolescent

```
                          -- H E R M A N N 8 --

Rorschach Sequence Report                                              Page   4
================================================================================

Card: I        Resp: 01  Rtn. Time:   0.00 W  o F       o    A          P
Card: I        Resp: 02  Rtn. Time:   7.80 W  o F       o    A                    PSV
Card: I        Resp: 03  Rtn. Time:  11.26 D  o F       -    Ge               >
Card: II       Resp: 04  Rtn. Time:   2.25 W  o FC      o    A            4.5
Card: II       Resp: 05  Rtn. Time:  13.13 DS o F       o    A
Card: III      Resp: 06  Rtn. Time:   3.35 D  o Ma      o (2) Hh.H     P
Card: IV       Resp: 07  Rtn. Time:  12.42 W  o mp.FD   o    (H)       P 2.0
Card: IV       Resp: 08  Rtn. Time:   4.78 W  o F       o    (A)         2.0      PSV
Card: V        Resp: 09  Rtn. Time:   2.69 W  o F       o    A          P 1.0 v
Card: V        Resp: 10  Rtn. Time:   8.02 W  o FC'     o    A            1.0 v
Card: VI       Resp: 11  Rtn. Time:  12.58 W  v F       u    Hh              v
Card: VII      Resp: 12  Rtn. Time:  25.10 D  o FT      o (2) A               v
Card: VIII     Resp: 13  Rtn. Time:  11.15 D  o FMa     o (2) A        P      >
Card: VIII     Resp: 14  Rtn. Time:   7.41 D  o ma.CF   u    Sc.Fi
Card: IX       Resp: 15  Rtn. Time:  18.56 D  o F       o    Ex              v
Card: X        Resp: 16  Rtn. Time:  11.37 D  o F       o    Hd
Card: X        Resp: 17  Rtn. Time:  10.87 D  o FC      o    (H).Cg      1.0   PSV.AB
```

EXHIBIT 8.1 (*Continued*)

Evaluation Report of a Suicidal Adolescent

```
                              -- H E R M A N N 8 --
Rorschach Structural Summary                                              Page   5
=================================================  =================================================
             n   %   Exner    Intl    Psych                   n   %   Exner    Intl    Psych
=================================================  =================================================
Global                                             Determinants
-------------------------------------------------  -------------------------------------------------
R            17                                     M            1   6
Rejects      0                                      FM           1   6   Low
P            5  29                                  m            2  12
(P)          0   0                                  FT           1   6
(2)          3  18                                  TF           0   0
Fr           0   0                                  T            0   0
rF           0   0                                  FY           0   0
3r+(2)       18                                     YF           0   0
RT Ach       9                                      Y            0   0
RT Ch        10                                     FV           0   0
AFR          42     High     High    High          VF           0   0
Zf           2      Low      Low                    V            0   0
ZSum         12                                     FC'          1   6
Zest         0                                      C'F          0   0
W            8  47                                  C'           0   0
D            9  53                                  FC           2  11
Dd           0   0                                  CF           1   6
DW           0   0                                  C            0   0
S            1   6                                  Cn           0   0
POSITION                                            FD           1   6
^            10 59                                  F            9  50
<            0   0                                  Blends       1   6
>            2  12                                  RATIOS
v            5  30                                  a            3  18
DEV QUAL                                            p            0   0
+            0   0                                  M            1   6   Low
o            16 94                                  wtd C        2
v/+          0   0                                  M+wtd C      3
v            1   6                                  FM+m         2
RATIOS                                              Y+T+V+C'     2
W            8                                      &FMmYTVC'    3
M            1   6   Low                            FC           2
W            8                                      CF+C         1
D            9
```

(*continues*)

EXHIBIT 8.1 *(Continued)*

Evaluation Report of a Suicidal Adolescent

```
                              -- H E R M A N N 8 --
  Rorschach Structural Summary                                              Page  6
  ======================================      ======================================
            n  %  Exner    Intl    Psych                n  %  Exner    Intl    Psych
  ======================================      ======================================
  Contents                                    Quality
  --------------------------------------      --------------------------------------
  CONT    8                                   OF ALL
  H       1  5  Low      Low     Low          +      0  0
  (H)     2  9                                o     14 82
  Hd      1  5                                u      2 12
  (Hd)    0  0                                -      1  6
  Hx      0  0                                none   0  0
  A       8 36                                OF F
  (A)     1  5                                +      0  0
  Ad      0  0  Low                           o      7 78  Low
  (Ad)    0  0                                u      1 11
  Ab      0  0                                -      1 11
  Al      0  0                                none   0  0
  An      0  0                                OF S
  Art     0  0                                +      0  0
  Ay      0  0                                o      1 100
  Bl      0  0                                u      0  0
  Bt      0  0                                -      0  0
  Cg      1  5                                none   0  0
  Cl      0  0                                SPECIAL SCORES
  Ex      1  5                                DV1    0  0
  Fi      1  5                                DV2    0  0
  Fd      0  0                                DR1    0  0
  Ge      1  5                                DR2    0  0
  Hh      2  9                                INC1   0  0
  Ls      0  0                                INC2   0  0
  Na      0  0                                FAB1   0  0
  Sc      1  5                                FAB2   0  0
  Sx      0  0                                ALOG   0  0
  Vo      0  0                                CON    0  0
  Xy      0  0                                AB     1  6
  Idio    0  0                                CP     0  0
  RATIOS                                      AG     0  0
  H+Hd    2                                   MOR    0  0
  A+Ad    8                                   CFB    0  0
  H+A     9                                   PER    0  0
  Hd+Ad   1                                   COP    0  0
  A%        41                                PSV    3 18  High     High    High
```

EXHIBIT 8.1 *(Continued)*

Evaluation Report of a Suicidal Adolescent

<hr>

REPORT OF PSYCHOLOGICAL EVALUATION

REPORT IN BRIEF: Susan (a pseudonym) is a 17-year-old adolescent who was admitted into the psychiatric ward after she cut her abdomen with a razor blade. The self-mutilation took place on Father's Day, apparently triggered by her feelings toward her father's death 3 years previously. The evaluation showed a great deal of repression and denial, an attempt to be strong and pull herself up by her bootstraps that has actually hindered her ability to work through her father's death. The result has been a depression that needed to be attended to at the time of the testing.

```
The Millon Adolescent Clinical Inventory (MACI)

    Personality Style Scales
    Scale  1. Introversive (Schizoid), Base Rate score....=   44
    Scale 2A. Inhibited (Avoidant).........................=   62
    Scale 2B. Doleful (Depressed)..........................=   34
    Scale  3. Submissive (Dependent).......................=   64
    Scale  4. Dramatizing (Histrionic).....................=   51
    Scale  5. Egotistic (Narcissistic).....................=   39
    Scale 6A. Unruly (Antisocial)..........................=   24
    Scale 6B. Forceful (Aggressive)........................=   12
    Scale  7. Conforming (Compulsive)......................=   66
    Scale 8A. Oppositional (Passive-aggressive/explosive).=   27
    Scale 8B. Self-Demeaning...............................=   53
    Scale  9. Borderline Tendency..........................=   21

    Expressed Concerns Scales
    Scale  A. Identity Diffusion...........................=   24
    Scale  B. Self-Devaluation.............................=   66
    Scale  C. Body Disapproval.............................=   61
    Scale  D. Sexual Discomfort............................=   63
    Scale  E. Peer Insecurity..............................=   51
    Scale  F. Social Insensitivity.........................=   32
    Scale  G. Family Discord...............................=   43
    Scale  H. Child Abuse..................................=    4

    Clinical Syndrome Scales
    Scale AA. Eating Dysfunctions..........................=   33
    Scale BB. Substance Abuse Proneness....................=   12
    Scale CC. Delinquent Predisposition....................=   19
    Scale DD. Impulsive Propensity.........................=   39
    Scale EE. Anxious Feelings.............................=   69
    Scale FF. Depressive Affect............................=   92 **
    Scale GG. Suicidal Tendency............................=   17

    Modifying Indices
    Scale  Y. Desirability.................................=   55
    Scale  Z. Debasement...................................=   47
    Scale  X. Disclosure...................................=   35
    Scale VV. Reliability..................................=    0
```

PERSONALITY ASSESSMENT: The scores that Susan obtained on the MACI were not significantly elevated in any of the personality scales. Statistically, the findings are nonsignificant, and there is nothing that can be said about her personality style. Nevertheless, it can be argued that Susan may be the type of person who does not have a characteristic style and does not have a ready-made, routine, or typical way in which she reacts to environmental events. Being this way may have the advantage of allowing her to readily vary her response in accordance to the situation that she is facing. It may have the disadvantage of preventing her from having an automatic response, a pattern of behavior that comes out naturally and predictably regardless of the situation at hand.

(continues)

EXHIBIT 8.1 (*Continued*)

Evaluation Report of a Suicidal Adolescent

EMOTIONAL ASSESSMENT: Consistent with the presenting complaints, the testing showed Susan to be depressed and dysphoric. Similar people are inclined to emphasize negative occurrences and to exhibit a melancholic mood and may be unlikely to experience much pleasure in life. They harbor a chronic sense of loss and feel hopeless about the prospect of making any significant changes in their lives. They typically have a low opinion of themselves. As shown by the Rorschach, the patient tended to be underproductive and to restrict her investment in the activities of her life. This was particularly remarkable given her history of being very involved and successful in sports and the student government. There is a certain suicide risk, as suggested by the following story given to Card 8GF of the Thematic Apperception Test:

> This one looks like a kid who's worried and looks like he's—there's a gun there, maybe he's—I don't know. He's worried about an operation he has to go to. Doesn't feel like doing it, maybe he feels like killing himself. There's—that's why there's a gun there, cause he doesn't want to go have an operation.

Perhaps here the "operation" symbolizes both the process Susan has to go through and the health issues that ended her father's life. Like the protagonist on Card 3, the patient is "upset" and "feel[ing] bad" because "something happened." But "she needs to learn how to deal with their emotions and work through stuff like this."

Judging from the test results, the way Susan has coped with adversity has been by denying or minimizing any issues and forging ahead. This coping strategy may have served her well in the past in that she has had many accomplishments, even after her father's death. These accomplishments have included reasonable academic achievements, good athletic endeavors, and many social successes such as her being elected class president.

The price paid for Susan's coping style is that of superficiality. The Rorschach characterized her as making little effort to organize or integrate information. Her perceptions may be referred to as naive or overly simplistic. This test pointed to her attempts to avoid affective or emotional stimuli as a means of dealing with her emotional experience. There was evidence that she may be excessively preoccupied with conventional behavior in a manner that tends to inhibit her creativity and originality. In this sense, this patient may be so concerned with finding the "correct" response that she frequently overlooks the more creative or original response.

Susan's superficiality and denial tendencies may have played a role in bringing about depressive symptoms. For one thing, she may not have been able to discuss losses, such as the death of her father, enough to have worked some of her feelings through. Feeling disconnected would have exacerbated any negative perceptions she had about herself. Moreover, according to the Rorschach, Susan tends to set unrealistically high goals, which may result in a chronic sense of frustration and disappointment. Finally, this test indicated the presence of low self-esteem, a problem that is typically accompanied by feelings of inferiority and inadequacy.

Seemingly because of Susan's coping style, the results of the self-report instruments were unrevealing. These scales mostly gave no elevations. The one telling exception was the elevation she obtained on the Depression Scale of the MACI. This elevation pointed to symptoms of depression including a decreased level of activity. Similar individuals experience a notable decrease in effectiveness, feelings of guilt and fatigue, and a tendency to be despairing about the future. Socially withdrawn, these people typically struggle with a loss of confidence and diminished feelings of adequacy and attractiveness.

In closing, Susan's many areas of strength should be emphasized. The patient had good contact with reality and did not demonstrate any psychopathology outside of the Mood Disorder symptoms.

Closing Remarks

Clinicians' reports are often the only part of their work that others see. These reports represent both a wonderful opportunity and a difficult responsibility. They must be professional, well formatted, and free of errors. They must also be interesting and informative. This is an area where we can offer you some guidance, but you have to develop your own style.

The Future of the Rorschach
What's in Store? 9

Any intelligent fool can make things bigger, more complex. . . . It takes a touch of genius—and a lot of courage to move in the opposite direction.
—E. F. Schumacher (1973, p. 22)

There has been a significant decline in graduate training on projective techniques in the United States, a diminution attributable to both insurance reimbursement policies and the recent negative attitudes toward projective assessment instruments (C. Piotrowski, 2015a, 2015b). Of the projective tests, the Rorschach, with its intricate scoring and the demands it makes for time and effort to learn and use, is most vulnerable. The second most widely used projective technique, the Thematic Apperception Test, is also in decline, but largely because of its psychodynamic heritage (C. Piotrowski, 2017). There are many countries (e.g., Spain) where the Rorschach is not taught in any of the universities (S. Scrimp, personal communication, November 12, 2016). Those of us who value this test have to find ways of adapting the instrument to the 21st century.

http://dx.doi.org/10.1037/0000075-010
Assessment Using the Rorschach Inkblot Test, by J. P. Choca and E. D. Rossini

Herm: An Abbreviated Rorschach Test

In our presentation at a meeting of the Society for Personality Assessment (SPA; Choca, Rossini, & Garside, 2016), we proposed reducing the number of cards administered. The inspiration came from our discovery of the Z Test (Zulliger & Salomon, 1970), a projective test with only three inkblots that is used in European and South American countries. Adapting that idea, we developed Herm (short for Hermann). Herm consists of only four of the standard Rorschach cards, two chromatic and two achromatic inkblots (Cards I, III, VI, and X). Using our archival data from 906 psychiatric patients, we compared 286 measures from the Comprehensive System (CS) Structural Summary on the four Herm cards to the same measures from the usual 10. The overall Pearson correlation was .94, the overall Spearman rank order correlation was .97, and all single correlations were significant at the .01 level or better.[1] To put these correlations in perspective, the temporal consistency (test–retest) correlations for the full test administered twice does not approach this level of equivalence (see table in Exner, 2003, p. 179). In other words, for all practical purposes, using Herm produced the same results as using the full Rorschach. Our results were consistent with similar conclusions about short versions reached by others (e.g., Carpenter et al., 1993; Grønnerød & Hartmann, 2010).

The discussant for our SPA presentation, Gregory J. Meyer, pointed to the obvious loss of information incurred when the Rorschach is shortened. He presented Rorschach Performance Assessment System (R-PAS) data comparing the results using the 10 cards with those derived from only five cards. The correlation for the Perceptual and Thinking Composite he presented was .91, and the validity of this composite decreased from .43 to .39; the correlation for human movement *(M)* was .86, with the validity decreasing from .35 to .29; and the test–retest correlation went from .59 to .53. The data obviously supported Meyer's point: Information is lost. And yet, we were thrilled with his data. If the reliability loss we have to accept for doing something in half the time is in the realm of .06, clinicians should not give another thought to using a Rorschach short form. You can use Herm with any scoring system you desire and simply multiply your obtained results by 2.5 for most variables.

A word of caution. There are many Rorschach variables that have a low frequency in the typical protocol. Some of these scores may be evoked by one of the cards Herm uses. Take, for instance, texture *(T)*. Many records have a *T (FT, TF,* or *T)* score of 1, a score frequently earned on Card VI (e.g., "furry animal skin rug" is the Popular response for this card). A *T* of 1 for a full Rorschach would be within the average range. Multiplying this score by 2.5 converts this score into an interpretable high marker. The problem

---

[1]The responses from the Herm sample were also included in the full 10-inkblot sample. We are well aware that this methodology inflated the correlations. The suggestion was made that we could compare the Herm sample with the responses given to the other six cards, but that would speak to the internal validity of the test, rather than the equivalence of Herm with the 10-card Rorschach. Sometime in the future we intend to do an equivalence study in which we give the Herm and the full Rorschach to the same individuals, using a counterbalanced design. Although that study would settle the question for sure, our current results argue against expecting any substantial differences.

would be solved if we had actual norms for Herm, but this project is in progress. In the meantime, those of us using Herm need to examine the variables that typically have a low score and make sure we are not converting them into interpretable high markers because of the 2.5 multiplier.

The Rorschach Centenarian Paradox

Old projectives never die; they simply fade away. We believe that the Rorschach will remain an assessment tool well into the future. However, without a partial return to its idiographic roots, it will become an increasingly specialized, technical tool used by fewer and fewer psychologists, perhaps to the point of near extinction. This is the Rorschach centenarian paradox. Approaching 100 years of continuous service, the Rorschach's scientific status is now unquestionable, and the CS and R-PAS rivalry provides considerable intellectual stimulation and wonderful teaching and learning opportunities at every level. The late Drs. Exner and Erard, as well as Drs. Meyer, Mihura, Viglione, Erdberg, Ritzler, and Sciara, are all on our American Rorschach Mount Rushmore! But as we asserted, both systems also share undesirable elements. We see both the CS and R-PAS as akin to the highly structured, lengthy, and mechanical psychiatric interviews used in research (e.g., Structured Clinical Interview for the *Diagnostic and Statistical Manual of Mental Disorders–5*; First, Williams, Benjamin, & Spitzer, 2016) but never used in actual clinical practice for the same reasons that make them so valuable in research.

In spite of its vitality within the Rorschach community, the other side of the centenarian paradox is its rapid decline in doctoral training, and ultimately in assessment practice as a consequence. We saw the same fate befall psychoanalytic psychology years ago when it was essentially eliminated from doctoral training programs and freestanding psychoanalytic institutes emerged in major cities (e.g., Center for Psychoanalytic Study in Chicago). We believe that divorcing the Rorschach from the universities and doctoral training programs for clinical psychologists is a mistake.

Our resolution to the centenarian paradox has one pragmatic remedy and one conceptual narrative. In keeping with E. F. Schumacher's quote, we are proposing a briefer and simpler approach to the Rorschach. This book addresses that need with Herm and a scaled-down coding system: the Basic Rorschach. In a timely and cost-effective manner, these developments may reverse the declining teaching and training trend.

Conceptually, new insights and fresh perspectives are greatly needed. We are heartened to see one on the horizon: the resurgence of female voices and feminist perspectives in the assessment profession and on the Rorschach specifically (Brabender & Mihura, 2016). These developments have the potential for redirecting the uses of the Rorschach to the assessment needs of the real psychological world, the world of interpersonal relatedness and its derivative psychopathologies (e.g., violence, oppression, abuse, trauma).

Closing Remarks

We have several hopes. First, we hope that this volume kindled your interest in studying the Rorschach in more detail from the CS perspective, the R-PAS perspective, our simplified perspective, or any other perspective that caught your fancy. Second, we hope that the practical recommendations we have offered will help save the Rorschach from extinction. No honest reader of the vast Rorschach literature can deny that the Rorschach is an important instrument in our clinical armamentarium, a powerful instrument capable of eliciting the personal uniqueness of the person before us. You are now part of that noble tradition.

Glossary

Both Rorschach scoring systems—the Comprehensive System (CS) and the Rorschach Performance Assessment System (R-PAS)—use abbreviations for most coded variables, as does the Basic Rorschach (BR) scoring system proposed in this book. The following is a list of codes and abbreviations, including some that are used by all systems and others that are unique to one system or the other. For the unique abbreviations, the system to which it applies is indicated in parentheses.

A. Whole animal (Content)
a. Active qualifier for movement (Determinant)
(A). Fictionalized whole animal (Content)
ABS. Abstract Representation (Special Score/Cognitive Code)
Ad. Animal detail or incomplete animal form (Content)
(Ad). Imaginary or fictional animal detail (Content)
Afr. Affective Ratio: *R* for last three cards / *R* for first seven cards
AG. Aggressive Content (Special Score, CS)
AGC. Aggressive Content (Cognitive Code, R-PAS)
AGM. Aggressive Movement (Cognitive Code, R-PAS)
ALOG. Alogic (Special Score, CS)
An. Anatomy; internal body parts not visible from outside (Content)
Art. Objects of art; paintings or decorative objects (Content)
Ay. Anthropology; objects with historical or cultural import (Content)
Bl. Blood (Content)
Blend. Response with more than one Determinant
Bt. Botany or plant (Content)

C. Color response with no form (Determinant)

C'. Any achromatic response (Determinant)

CF. Color-dominant form response (Determinant based on Content)

Cg. Clothing (Content)

Cl. Cloud (Content)

CON. Contamination (Special Score/Cognitive Code)

COP. Cooperative Movement (Special Score/Cognitive Code)

D. Large detail (Location)

d. Small detail; area smaller than 10% of the inkblot (BR)

Dd. Small detail

DQ. Developmental Quality (CS)

DR. Deviant Response (Special Score/Cognitive Code)

DV. Deviant Verbalization (Special Score/Cognitive Code)

Ex. Explosion (Content)

F. Response with no other Determinant

F%. $(F / R) * 100$

F–%. $(F$ responses with $FQ– / R) * 100$

FAB. Fabulized Combination (Special Score/Cognitive Code)

FC. Form-dominant color response (Determinant based on Content)

FD. Form Dimension (Determinant)

Fd. Food (Content)

Fi. Fire (Content)

FM. Animal movement (Determinant)

FQ. Form Quality

FQX. Form Quality level of all responses

Fr. Reflection (Determinant)

Ge. Geography, such as a map (Content)

H. Human content (Content)

(H). Fictionalized human content (Content)

Hd. Human detail or incomplete human figure (Content)

(Hd). Imaginary or fictional human detail (Content)

Hh. Household object (Content)

Hx. Human experience, such as emotion (Content)

Idio. Content not classified in other categories

INC. Incongruous Combination (Special Score/Cognitive Code)

Lambda. Proportion of *F* to non-*F* responses: $L = F / R – F$

Ls. Landscape (Content)

M. Human movement (Determinant)

m. Inanimate movement (Determinant)

MAH. Mutuality of Autonomy—Health (Special Score/Cognitive Code)

MAP. Mutuality of Autonomy—Pathology (Special Score/Cognitive Code)

MOA. Mutuality of Autonomy Scale (R-PAS)

MOR. Morbid Response (Special Score/Cognitive Code)

MQ–. Number of human movement responses of negative (–) Form Quality

Na. Nature (Content)

NB. Nota bene to flag any other aspect that needs attention (BR)

Nc. Content not classified in other categories (R-PAS)

NPH. Non-Pure-Human responses: *(H) + Hd + (Hd)* (R-PAS)

o. Response consistent with shape of inkblot (Form Quality)

Ob. Human-made object (BR)

ODL. Oral Dependent Language (Special Score/Cognitive Code)

P. Popular response

p. Passive qualifier for movement Determinant

PEC. Peculiar Logic (Cognitive Code, R-PAS)

PER. Personal Knowledge (Special Score/Cognitive Code)

PHR. Poor Human Representation (R-PAS)

PV. Pathological Verbalization (Special Score/Cognitive Code)

R. Number of responses

S. Use of white space or significant reversal of the figure–ground perspective (Location)

S–%. (*S* responses with *FQ– / R*) * 100

Sc. Science (Content)

SumC. *FC + CF + C* (Determinant)

SumC'. *FC' + C'F + C'* (Determinant)

SumH. *H + Hd + (H) + (Hd)* (Content)

Sum6. Six Special Score/Cognitive Codes Sum: *DV + DR + INC + FAB + CON + ALOG*

SumT. *FT + TF + T* (Determinant)

SumV. *FV + VF + V* (Determinant)

SumY. *FY + YF + Y* (Determinant)

Sx. Sexual organs or activity or sexy clothing (Content)

T. Texture response (Determinant)

u. Content marginally consistent with shape of inkblot (Form Quality)

V. Vista response (Determinant)

W. Response using the whole inkblot (Location)

WSumC. Weighted *SumC*: 0.5 * *FC + CF +* 1.5 * *C*

WSum6. Weighted *Sum6*: *Sum6* scores with Level 2 scores multiplied by 2

X–%. Total percentage of responses with poor Form Quality

Xy. X-ray (Content)

Y. Shading response (Determinant)

Zf. Pairs

–. Content not consistent with shape of inkblot

References

Acklin, M. W. (1992). Psychodiagnosis of personality structure: Psychotic personality organization. *Journal of Personality Assessment, 58,* 454–463. http://dx.doi.org/10.1207/s15327752jpa5803_2

Acklin, M. W. (1993). Psychodiagnosis of personality structure II: Borderline personality organization. *Journal of Personality Assessment, 61,* 329–341. http://dx.doi.org/10.1207/s15327752jpa6102_13

Acklin, M. W. (1994). Psychodiagnosis of personality structure III: Neurotic personality organization. *Journal of Personality Assessment, 63,* 1–9. http://dx.doi.org/10.1207/s15327752jpa6301_1

"Airplane crash-lands into Hudson River; all aboard reported safe." (2009, January 15). *CNN.* Retrieved from http://www.cnn.com/2009/US/01/15/new.york.plane.crash/

American Psychiatric Association. (2013). *Diagnostic and statistical manual of mental disorders* (5th ed.). Arlington, VA: Author.

Ames, L. B., Métraux, R. W., Rodell, J. L., & Walker, R. N. (1973). *Rorschach responses in old age* (rev. ed.). Oxford, England: Brunner/Mazel.

Ames, L. B., Métraux, R. W., Rodell, J. L., & Walker, R. N. (1974). *Child Rorschach responses* (rev. ed.). New York, NY: Brunner-Mazel.

Aronow, E., & Reznikoff, M. (1976). *Rorschach content interpretation.* New York, NY: Grune & Stratton.

Aronow, E., Reznikoff, M., & Moreland, K. (1994). *The Rorschach technique.* Boston, MA: Allyn & Bacon.

Baity, M. R., & Hilsenroth, M. J. (2002). Rorschach Aggressive Content (AgC) variable: A study of criterion validity. *Journal of Personality Assessment, 78,* 275–287. http://dx.doi.org/10.1207/S15327752JPA7802_04

Baldessarini, R. J., Finklestein, S., & Arana, G. W. (1983). The predictive power of diagnostic tests and the effect of prevalence of illness. *Archives of General Psychiatry, 40,* 569–573. http://dx.doi.org/10.1001/archpsyc.1983.01790050095011

Bartell, S. S., & Solanto, M. V. (1995). Usefulness of the Rorschach inkblot test in assessment of attention deficit hyperactivity disorder. *Perceptual and Motor Skills, 80,* 531–541. http://dx.doi.org/10.2466/pms.1995.80.2.531

Beck, S. J. (1950). *Rorschach's test, basic processes.* New York, NY: Grune & Stratton.

Beck, S. J. (1976). *The Rorschach test exemplified in classics of drama and fiction.* New York, NY: Stratton Intercontinental Medical Book.

Blackall, G. F. (1995). A descriptive study of the personality structure of pediatric leukemia survivors. *Dissertation Abstracts International: Section B. Sciences and Engineering, 56,* 2315.

Blais, M. A., & Hilsenroth, M. J. (1998). Rorschach correlates of the *DSM–IV* histrionic personality disorder. *Journal of Personality Assessment, 70,* 355–364. http://dx.doi.org/10.1207/s15327752jpa7002_12

Blais, M. A., Hilsenroth, M. J., Castlebury, F., Fowler, J. C., & Baity, M. R. (2001). Predicting *DSM–IV* Cluster B personality disorder criteria from MMPI–2 and Rorschach data: A test of incremental validity. *Journal of Personality Assessment, 76,* 150–168. http://dx.doi.org/10.1207/S15327752JPA7601_9

Blatt, S. J., & Ford, R. Q. (1994). *Therapeutic change: An object relations perspective.* New York, NY: Plenum Press.

Bornstein, R. F. (2005). The dependent patient: Diagnosis, assessment, and treatment. *Professional Psychology: Research and Practice, 36,* 82–89. http://dx.doi.org/10.1037/0735-7028.36.1.82

Bornstein, R. F., & Masling, J. M. (2005). *Scoring the Rorschach: Seven validated systems.* Mahwah, NJ: Erlbaum.

Brabender, V. M., & Mihura, J. L. (2016). *Handbook of gender and sexuality in psychological assessment.* New York, NY: Routledge/Taylor & Francis.

Brainard, R. B. (2005). A comparison of learning-disabled children and non–learning-disabled children on the Rorschach: An information processing perspective. *Dissertation Abstracts International: Section B. Sciences and Engineering, 65,* 6643.

Bram, A., & Peebles, M. J. (2014). *Psychological testing that matters: Creating a road map for effective treatment.* Washington, DC: American Psychological Association. http://dx.doi.org/10.1037/14340-000

Brand, B. L., Armstrong, J. G., Loewenstein, R. J., & McNary, S. W. (2009). Personality differences on the Rorschach of dissociative identity disorder, borderline personality disorder, and psychotic inpatients. *Psychological Trauma: Theory, Research, Practice, and Policy, 1,* 188–205. http://dx.doi.org/10.1037/a0016561

Butcher, J. N., Dahlstrom, E. G., Graham, J. R., Tellegen, A., & Kaemmer, B. (1989). *Minnesota Multiphasic Personality Inventory—2 (MMPI–2): Manual for administration and scoring.* Minneapolis: University of Minnesota Press.

Campo, V. (2008). Cultura y Rorschach: Las respuestas populares [Culture and Rorschach: The Popular responses]. *Revista de la Sociedad Española del Rorschach y Métodos Proyectivos, 23,* 25–38.

Caplan, R., Guthrie, D., Tang, B., Nuechterlein, K. H., & Asarnow, R. E. (2001). Thought disorder in attention-deficit hyperactivity disorder. *Journal of the American Academy of Child & Adolescent Psychiatry, 40,* 965–972. http://dx.doi.org/10.1097/00004583-200108000-00019

Carpenter, J. T., Coleman, M. J., Waternaux, C. M., Perry, J., Wong, H., O'Brian, C., & Holtzman, P. S. (1993). The Thought Disorder Index: Short form assessments. *Psychological Assessment, 5,* 75–80. http://dx.doi.org/10.1037/1040-3590.5.1.75

Carroll, G., Giler, D., Hill, W. (Producers), & Scott, R. (Director). (1979). *Alien* [Motion picture]. United States: 20th Century Fox.

Carroll, L. (1871). The walrus and the carpenter. In *Through the looking glass: And what Alice found there.* London, England: Macmillan.

Cassella, M. J. (1999). The Rorschach texture response: A conceptual validation study. *Dissertation Abstracts International: Section B. Sciences and Engineering, 60,* 2405.

Chekhov, A. (1993). Ward no. 6. In S. Foote (Ed.) & C. Garnett (Trans.), *Longer stories from the last decade* (pp. 146–198). New York, NY: Random House. (Original work published 1892)

Choca, J. P. (2004). *Interpretive guide to the Millon Clinical Multiaxial Inventory* (3rd ed.). Washington, DC: American Psychological Association.

Choca, J. P. (2013). *The Rorschach Inkblot Test: An interpretive guide for clinicians.* Washington, DC: American Psychological Association. http://dx.doi.org/10.1037/14039-000

Choca, J. P. (2015, March). *The future of the Rorschach: Reclaiming the test from the empiricist's pawnshop.* Paper presented at the meeting of the Society for Personality Assessment, Brooklyn, NY.

Choca, J. P. (2017). *Hermann: A Rorschach administration and scoring assistant* (10th ed.) [Computer program].

Choca, J. P., Rossini, E. D., & Garside, D. (2016, March). *The practical Rorschach: Adapting the Rorschach to the 21st century.* Symposium conducted at the meeting of the Society for Personality Assessment, Chicago, IL.

Choca, J. P., Van Denburg, E., & Mouton, A. (1994, March). *Time for a new look at an old Rorschach marker: Reaction times collected with the Hermann computer program.* Paper presented at the meeting of the Society for Personality Assessment, Chicago, IL.

Cocking, R. R., Dana, J. M., & Dana, R. H. (1969). Six constructs to define Rorschach *M*: A response. *Journal of Projective Techniques & Personality Assessment, 33,* 322–323. http://dx.doi.org/10.1080/0091651X.1969.10380155

Conti, R. P. (2007). The concealment of psychopathology on the Rorschach in criminal forensic evaluations. *Dissertation Abstracts International: Section B. Sciences and Engineering, 68,* 4125.

De Carolis, A., & Ferracuti, S. (2005). Correlation between the Rorschach test coded and interpreted according to the Comprehensive Exner System and the Eysenck Personality Inventory. *Rorschachiana, 27,* 63–79. http://dx.doi.org/10.1027/1192-5604.27.1.63

de Ruiter, C., & Cohen, L. (1992). Personality in panic disorder with agoraphobia: A Rorschach study. *Journal of Personality Assessment, 59,* 304–316. http://dx.doi.org/10.1207/s15327752jpa5902_7

Draguns, J. G., Haley, E. M., & Phillips, L. (1967). Studies of Rorschach content: A review of the research literature. 1. Traditional content categories. *Journal of Projective Techniques & Personality Assessment, 31*, 3–32. http://dx.doi.org/10.1080/0091651X.1967.10120338

Eastwood, C., Marshall, F., Stewart, A., Moore, T. (Producers), & Eastwood, C. (Director). (2016). *Sully* [Motion picture]. United States: Warner Bros.

Egozi-Profeta, V. L. (1999). A comparison of the Roemer and the Rorschach tests as tools for distinguishing characteristics of psychopathy. *Dissertation Abstracts International: Section B. Sciences and Engineering, 60*, 1345.

Elfhag, K., Barkeling, B., Carlsson, A. M., Lindgren, T., & Rössner, S. (2004). Food intake with an antiobesity drug (sibutramine) versus placebo and Rorschach data: A crossover within-subjects study. *Journal of Personality Assessment, 82*, 158–168. http://dx.doi.org/10.1207/s15327752jpa8202_4

Exner, J. E., Jr. (1962). The effect of color on productivity in Cards VIII, IX, X of the Rorschach. *Journal of Projective Techniques, 26*, 30–33. http://dx.doi.org/10.1080/08853126.1962.10381074

Exner, J. E., Jr. (1974). *The Rorschach: A comprehensive system: Vol. 1. Basic foundations*. New York, NY: Wiley.

Exner, J. E., Jr. (1993). *The Rorschach: A comprehensive system* (3rd ed., Vol. 1). New York, NY: Wiley.

Exner, J. E., Jr. (2003). *The Rorschach: A comprehensive system* (4th ed., Vol. 1). New York, NY: Wiley.

Exner, J. E., Jr. (2007). A new U.S. adult nonpatient sample. *Journal of Personality Assessment, 89*(Suppl. 1), S154–S158. http://dx.doi.org/10.1080/00223890701583523

Exner, J. E., Jr., Colligan, S. C., Boll, T. J., Stischer, B., & Hillman, L. (1996). Rorschach findings concerning closed head injury patients. *Assessment, 3*, 317–326. http://dx.doi.org/10.1177/1073191196003003011

Exner, J. E., Jr., Thomas, E. A., & Mason, B. (1985). Children's Rorschachs: Description and prediction. *Journal of Personality Assessment, 49*, 13–20. http://dx.doi.org/10.1207/s15327752jpa4901_3

Exner, J. E., Jr., & Wylie, J. (1977). Some Rorschach data concerning suicide. *Journal of Personality Assessment, 41*, 339–348. http://dx.doi.org/10.1207/s15327752jpa4104_1

Finn, S. E. (1996). Assessment feedback integrating MMPI–2 and Rorschach findings. *Journal of Personality Assessment, 67*, 543–557. http://dx.doi.org/10.1207/s15327752jpa6703_10

Finn, S. E., Fischer, C. T., & Handler, L. (2012). *Collaborative/therapeutic assessment: A casebook and guide*. Hoboken, NJ: Wiley.

First, M. B., Williams, J. B., Benjamin, L. S., & Spitzer, R. L. (2016). *Structured clinical interview for the DSM–5*. Arlington, VA: American Psychiatric Association.

Fowler, J. C., Brunnschweiler, B., Swales, S., & Brock, J. (2005). Assessment of Rorschach dependency measures in female inpatients diagnosed with borderline personality disorder. *Journal of Personality Assessment, 85*, 146–153. http://dx.doi.org/10.1207/s15327752jpa8502_07

Frank, G. (1992). The response of African Americans to the Rorschach: A review of the research. *Journal of Personality Assessment, 59,* 317–325. http://dx.doi.org/10.1207/s15327752jpa5902_8

Fúster, J. (2008). Adaptar el Rorschach a la población española [Adapting the Rorschach to the Spanish population]. *Revista de la Sociedad Española del Rorschach y Métodos Proyectivos, 23,* 54–67.

Fúster, J., & Campo, V. (2010). Normas que reflejan la singularidad: La necesidad de adaptar los valores del SC a cada país [Norms that reflect singularity: The need to adapt CS values for each country]. *Revista de la Sociedad Española del Rorschach y Métodos Proyectivos, 23,* 45–56.

Gacono, C. B., & Evans, F. B. (2008). *The handbook of forensic Rorschach assessment.* New York, NY: Routledge.

Gacono, C. B., Gacono, L. A., Meloy, J. R., & Baity, M. R. (2008). The Rorschach assessment of aggression: The Rorschach Extended Aggression Scores. In C. B. Gacono & F. B. Evans (Eds.), *The handbook of forensic Rorschach assessment* (pp. 543–559). New York, NY: Routledge.

Gacono, C. B., & Meloy, J. R. (1991). A Rorschach investigation of attachment and anxiety in antisocial personality disorder. *Journal of Nervous and Mental Disease, 179,* 546–552. http://dx.doi.org/10.1097/00005053-199109000-00005

Gacono, C. B., Meloy, J. R., & Heaven, T. R. (1990). A Rorschach investigation of narcissism and hysteria in antisocial personality. *Journal of Personality Assessment, 55,* 270–279. http://dx.doi.org/10.1080/00223891.1990.9674066

Ganellen, R. J. (1996). *Integrating the Rorschach and the MMPI–2 in personality assessment.* Hillsdale, NJ: Erlbaum.

Ganellen, R. J. (2008). Rorschach assessment of malingering and defense response sets. In C. B. Gacono & F. B. Evans (Eds.), *The handbook of forensic Rorschach assessment* (pp. 89–120). New York, NY: Routledge.

Gardner, R. W. (1951). Impulsivity as indicated by Rorschach test factors. *Journal of Consulting Psychology, 15,* 464–468. http://dx.doi.org/10.1037/h0061368

Gerard-Sharp, S. (2000). A Rorschach study of interpersonal disturbance in priest same-sex ephebophiles. *Dissertation Abstracts International: Section B. Sciences and Engineering, 61,* 2199.

Goldman, G. N. (2001). Rorschach variables as indicators of depression in an inpatient adolescent population. *Dissertation Abstracts International: Section B. Sciences and Engineering, 62,* 2483.

Goncharov, I. (1915). *Oblomov* (C. J. Hogarth, Trans.). New York, NY: Macmillan. (Original work published 1859)

Graceffo, R. A., Mihura, J. L., & Meyer, G. J. (2014). A meta-analysis of an implicit measure of personality functioning: The Mutuality of Autonomy Scale. *Journal of Personality Assessment, 96,* 581–595. http://dx.doi.org/10.1080/00223891.2014.919299

Greenwald, D. F. (1990). An external construct validity study of Rorschach personality variables. *Journal of Personality Assessment, 55,* 768–780. http://dx.doi.org/10.1080/00223891.1990.9674111

Greenwald, D. F. (1999). Relationships between the Rorschach and the NEO—Five Factor Inventory. *Psychological Reports, 85,* 519–527. http://dx.doi.org/10.2466/pr0.1999.85.2.519

Grønnerød, C., & Hartmann, E. (2010). Moving Rorschach scoring forward: The RN—Rorschach Scoring System as an exemplar of simplified scoring. *Rorschachiana, 31,* 22–42. http://dx.doi.org/10.1027/1192-5604/a000003

Gussow, M., & Holditch, K. (Eds.). (2000). *Tennessee Williams: Plays 1937–1955.* New York, NY: Library of America.

Harrower, M., & Bowers, D. (1987). *The inside story: Self-evaluations reflecting basic Rorschach types.* Hillsdale, NJ: Erlbaum.

Hartmann, E. (2001). Rorschach administration: A comparison of the effect of two instructions. *Journal of Personality Assessment, 76,* 461–471. http://dx.doi.org/10.1207/S15327752JPA7603_07

Hartmann, E., & Vanem, P. C. (2003). Rorschach administration: A comparison of the effect of two instructions given to an inpatient sample of drug addicts. *Scandinavian Journal of Psychology, 44,* 133–139. http://dx.doi.org/10.1111/1467-9450.00331

Holaday, M. (1998). Rorschach protocols of children and adolescents with severe burns: A follow-up study. *Journal of Personality Assessment, 71,* 306–321. http://dx.doi.org/10.1207/s15327752jpa7103_2

Holaday, M., Moak, J., & Shipley, M. A. (2001). Rorschach protocols from children and adolescents with Asperger's disorder. *Journal of Personality Assessment, 76,* 482–495. http://dx.doi.org/10.1207/S15327752JPA7603_09

Horn, S. L., Meyer, G. J., & Mihura, J. L. (2009). Impact of card rotation on the frequency of Rorschach reflection responses. *Journal of Personality Assessment, 91,* 346–356. http://dx.doi.org/10.1080/00223890902936090

Huprich, S. K. (2006). *Rorschach assessment of the personality disorders.* Mahwah, NJ: Erlbaum.

Hutt, M. L., & Shor, J. (1946). Rationale for routine Rorschach "testing the limits." *Rorschach Research Exchange, 10,* 70–76. http://dx.doi.org/10.1080/08934037.1946.10381180

İkiz, T. (2011). The history and development of the Rorschach test in Turkey. *Rorschachiana, 32,* 72–90. http://dx.doi.org/10.1027/1192-5604/a000016

Kernberg, O. F. (1984). *Severe personality disorders: Psychotherapeutic strategies.* New Haven, CT: Yale University Press.

King, D. B., Viney, W., & Woody, W. D. (2013). *A history of psychology: Ideas and context* (5th ed.). Boston, MA: Allyn & Bacon.

Kleiger, J. H. (1999). *Disordered thinking and the Rorschach: Theory, research, and differential diagnosis.* Hillsdale, NJ: Analytic Press.

Kleiger, J. H. (2015). An open letter to Hermann Rorschach: What has become of your experiment? *Rorschachiana, 36,* 221–241. http://dx.doi.org/10.1027/1192-5604/a000071

Klopfer, B., Ainsworth, M. D., Klopfer, W., & Holt, R. R. (1954). *Developments in the Rorschach technique* (Vol. 1). New York, NY: Harcourt.

Kobler, F. J. (1983). The Rorschach test in clinical practice. *Interdisciplinaria: Revista de Psicología y Ciencias Afines, 4,* 131–139.

Kochinski, S., Smith, S. R., Baity, M. R., & Hilsenroth, M. J. (2008). Rorschach correlates of adolescent self-mutilation. *Bulletin of the Menninger Clinic, 72*, 54–77. http://dx.doi.org/10.1521/bumc.2008.72.1.54

Kvaal, S., Choca, J., Groth-Marnat, G., & Davis, A. (2011). The integrated psychological report. In T. M. Harwood, L. E. Beutler, & G. Groth-Marnat (Eds.), *Integrated assessment of adult personality* (3rd ed., pp. 413–444). New York, NY: Guilford Press.

Lamounier, R., & de Villemor-Amaral, A. E. (2006). Evidence of validity for the Rorschach in the context of traffic psychology. *Revista Interamericana de Psicología, 40*, 167–176.

Lee, H. J., Kim, Z. S., & Kwon, S. M. (2005). Thought disorder in patients with obsessive–compulsive disorder. *Journal of Clinical Psychology, 61*, 401–413. http://dx.doi.org/10.1002/jclp.20115

Leichtman, M. (2004). Projective tests: The nature of the task. In M. J. Hilsenroth & D. L. Segal (Eds.), *Comprehensive handbook of psychological assessment* (Vol. 2, pp. 297–314). Hoboken, NJ: Wiley.

Loving, J. L., Jr., & Russell, W. F. (2000). Selected Rorschach variables of psychopathic juvenile offenders. *Journal of Personality Assessment, 75*, 126–142. http://dx.doi.org/10.1207/S15327752JPA7501_9

Lunazzi, H. A. (2015). Presentación de las normas regionales de Argentina para la técnica Rorschach [Presentation of regional norms for Argentina for the Rorschach technique]. *Psicodiagnosticar, 25*, 27–44.

Malone, J. C., Stein, M. B., Slavin-Mulford, J., Bello, I., Sinclair, S. J., & Blais, M. A. (2013). Seeing red: Affect modulation and chromatic color responses on the Rorschach. *Bulletin of the Menninger Clinic, 77*, 70–93.

Mann, T. (1936). Tobias Mindernickel. In H. T. Lowe-Porter (Trans.), *Stories of three decades* (pp. 51–57). New York, NY: Knopf. (Original work published 1898)

Masling, J., Rabie, L., & Blondheim, S. H. (1967). Obesity, level of aspiration, and Rorschach and TAT measures of oral dependence. *Journal of Consulting Psychology, 31*, 233–239. http://dx.doi.org/10.1037/h0020999

McAdams, D. P. (1994). A psychology of a stranger. *Psychological Inquiry, 5*, 145–148. http://dx.doi.org/10.1207/s15327965pli0502_12

McCarroll, B. R. (1998). Caregiving disruptions and attachment in psychiatric inpatient adolescents. *Dissertation Abstracts International: Section B. Sciences and Engineering, 59*, 2457.

Mearns, W. H. (2000). Antigonish. In J. R. Colombo (Ed.), *Ghost stories of Canada* (p. 46). Toronto, Ontario, Canada: Dundurn. (Original work published 1899)

Meloy, J. R. (1992). Revisiting the Rorschach of Sirhan Sirhan. *Journal of Personality Assessment, 58*, 548–570. http://dx.doi.org/10.1207/s15327752jpa5803_10

Meloy, J. R., Acklin, M. W., Gacono, C. B., Murray, J. F., & Peterson, C. A. (1997). *Contemporary Rorschach interpretation*. Mahwah, NJ: Erlbaum.

Mesirow, T. R. (1999). Self-mutilation: Analysis of a psychiatric forensic population. *Dissertation Abstracts International: Section B. Sciences and Engineering, 60*, 2354.

Meyer, G. J., Erdberg, P., & Shaffer, T. W. (2007). Toward international normative reference data for the Comprehensive System. *Journal of Personality Assessment, 89*(Suppl. 1), S201–S216. http://dx.doi.org/10.1080/00223890701629342

Meyer, G. J., Giromini, L., Viglione, D. J., Reese, J. B., & Mihura, J. L. (2015). The association of gender, ethnicity, age, and education with Rorschach scores. *Assessment, 22*, 46–64. http://dx.doi.org/10.1177/1073191114544358

Meyer, G. J., Viglione, D. J., Mihura, J. L., Erard, R. E., & Erdberg, P. (2011). *Rorschach performance assessment system*. Toledo, OH: Rorschach Performance Assessment System.

Mihura, J. L., Meyer, G. J., Dumitrascu, N., & Bombel, G. (2013). The validity of individual Rorschach variables: Systematic reviews and meta-analyses of the Comprehensive System. *Psychological Bulletin, 139*, 548–605. http://dx.doi.org/10.1037/a0029406

Mihura, J. L., Nathan-Montano, E., & Alperin, R. J. (2003). Rorschach measures of aggressive drive derivatives: A college student sample. *Journal of Personality Assessment, 80*, 41–49. http://dx.doi.org/10.1207/S15327752JPA8001_12

Mihura, J. L., Roy, M., & Graceffo, R. A. (2017). Psychological assessment training in clinical psychology doctoral programs. *Journal of Personality Assessment, 99*, 153–164. http://dx.doi.org/10.1080/00223891.2016.1201978

Miller, T. A. (1999). Rorschach assessment of object relations and affect control in domestic violent and non-violent couples. *Dissertation Abstracts International: Section A. Humanities and Social Sciences, 59*, 4069.

Millon, T. A. (1990). *Toward a new personology: An evolutionary model*. New York, NY: Wiley.

Millon, T. A. (2016). *MCMI–IV manual*. Minneapolis, MN: National Computer Systems.

Mindess, H. (1970). The symbolic dimension. In B. Klopfer, M. M. Meyer, F. B. Brawer, & W. G. Klopfer (Eds.), *Developments in the Rorschach technique* (Vol. 3, pp. 83–97). New York, NY: Harcourt Brace Jovanovich.

Morey, L. (1991). *Personality assessment inventory*. Lutz, FL: Psychological Assessment Resources.

Mulder, J. L. (1997). Assessment of emotionally disturbed adolescents using the Rorschach: An analysis of the *EA/es* relationship. *Dissertation Abstracts International: Section A. Humanities and Social Sciences, 58*, 1200.

Muñoz, C., Choca, J., Rossini, E., & Garside, D. (2011, March). *Psychiatric norms for the Rorschach*. Paper presented at the meeting of the Society for Personality Assessment, Boston, MA.

Murray, H. A. (1938). *Explorations in personality*. New York, NY: Oxford University Press.

Murray, H. A. (1943). *Thematic apperception test*. Cambridge, MA: Harvard University Press.

Murray, J. F. (1992). Toward a synthetic approach to the Rorschach: The case of a psychotic child. *Journal of Personality Assessment, 58*, 494–505. http://dx.doi.org/10.1207/s15327752jpa5803_5

Nezworski, M. T., & Wood, J. M. (1995). Narcissism in the Comprehensive System for the Rorschach. *Clinical Psychology: Science and Practice, 2*, 179–199. http://dx.doi.org/10.1111/j.1468-2850.1995.tb00038.x

Ogdon, D. P. (2001). *Psychodiagnostics and personality assessment: A handbook*. Los Angeles, CA: Western Psychological Services.

Osher, Y., & Bersudsky, Y. (2007). Thought disorder in euthymic bipolar patients: A possible endophenotype of bipolar affective disorder? *Journal of Nervous and Mental Disease, 195*, 857–860. http://dx.doi.org/10.1097/NMD.0b013e318156832d

Paul, A. M. (2004). *The cult of personality testing*. New York, NY: Free Press.

Perry, W., & Potterat, E. (1997). Beyond personality assessment: The use of the Rorschach as a neuropsychological instrument in patients with amnestic disorders. In J. R. Meloy, M. W. Acklin, C. B. Gacono, J. F. Murray, & C. A. Peterson (Eds.), *Contemporary Rorschach interpretation* (pp. 557–575). Mahwah, NJ: Erlbaum.

Perry, W., Potterat, E., Auslander, L., Kaplan, E., & Jeste, D. (1996). A neuropsychological approach to the Rorschach in patients with dementia of the Alzheimer type. *Assessment, 3*, 351–363. http://dx.doi.org/10.1177/1073191196003003014

Peterson, C. A. (2010). The encounter with the unfamiliar. *Rorschachiana, 31*, 90–111. http://dx.doi.org/10.1027/1192-5604/a000006

Peterson, C. A., & Horowitz, M. (1990). Perceptual robustness of the nonrelationship between psychopathology and popular responses on the Hand Test and the Rorschach. *Journal of Personality Assessment, 54*, 415–418. http://dx.doi.org/10.1207/s15327752jpa5401&2_38

Petot, J. M. (2005). Are the relationships between NEO PI-R and Rorschach markers of openness to experience dependent on the patient's test-taking attitude? *Rorschachiana, 27*, 30–50. http://dx.doi.org/10.1027/1192-5604.27.1.30

Petrosky, E. M. (2005). The relationship between the morbid response of the Rorschach inkblot test and self-reported depressive symptomatology. *SIS Journal of Projective Psychology & Mental Health, 12*, 87–98.

Phillips, L., & Smith, J. G. (1953). *Rorschach interpretation: Advanced technique*. New York, NY: Grune & Stratton.

Piotrowski, C. (2015a). Clinical instruction on projective techniques in the USA: A review of academic training settings 1995–2014. *SIS Journal of Projective Psychology & Mental Health, 22*, 83–92.

Piotrowski, C. (2015b). On the decline of projective techniques in professional psychology training. *North American Journal of Psychology, 17*, 259–266.

Piotrowski, C. (2017). Thematic apperception techniques (TAT, CAT) in assessment: A summary review of 67 survey-based studies of training and professional settings. *SIS Journal of Projective Psychology & Mental Health, 24*, 3–17.

Piotrowski, Z. (1937). The Rorschach inkblot method in organic disturbances of the central nervous system. *Journal of Nervous and Mental Disease, 86*, 525–537. http://dx.doi.org/10.1097/00005053-193711000-00002

Potkay, C. R. (1971). *The Rorschach clinician: A new research approach and its application*. New York, NY: Grune & Stratton.

Priyamvada, R., Kumari, S., Ranjan, R., Prakash, J., Singh, A., & Chaudhury, S. (2009). Rorschach profile of schizophrenia and depression. *SIS Journal of Projective Psychology & Mental Health, 16*, 37–40.

Rapaport, D., Gill, M., & Schafer, R. (1968). *Diagnostic psychological testing* (rev. ed., pp. 268–463). New York, NY: International Universities Press.

Ray, A. B. (1963). Juvenile delinquency by Rorschach inkblots. *Psychologia, 6*, 190–192.

Rorschach, H. (1942). *Psychodiagnostics: A diagnostic test based on perception* (P. Lemkau & B. Kronenberg, Trans.). Bern, Switzerland: Hans Huber. (Original work published 1921)

Rose, T., Kaser-Boyd, N., & Maloney, M. P. (2001). *Essentials of Rorschach assessment.* Hoboken, NJ: Wiley.

Rossini, E. D., & Moretti, R. J. (1997). Thematic Apperception Test (TAT) interpretation: Practice recommendations from a survey of clinical psychology doctoral programs accredited by the American Psychological Association. *Professional Psychology: Research and Practice, 28,* 393–398. http://dx.doi.org/10.1037/0735-7028.28.4.393

Roth, P. (1959, March 14). Defender of the faith. *The New Yorker,* pp. 44–50.

Ryan, G. P., Baerwald, J. P., & McGlone, G. (2008). Cognitive mediational deficits and the role of coping styles in pedophile and ephebophile Roman Catholic clergy. *Journal of Clinical Psychology, 64,* 1–16. http://dx.doi.org/10.1002/jclp.20428

Schafer, R. (1948). *Clinical applications of psychological tests.* New York, NY: International Universities Press.

Schafer, R. (1954). *Psychoanalytic interpretation in Rorschach testing.* New York, NY: Grune & Stratton.

Schneider, R. B., Huprich, S. K., & Fuller, K. M. (2008). The Rorschach and the Inventory of Interpersonal Problems. *Rorschachiana, 29,* 3–24. http://dx.doi.org/10.1027/1192-5604.29.1.3

Schultz, D. S., & Loving, J. L. (2012). Challenges since Wikipedia: The availability of Rorschach information online and Internet users' reactions to online media coverage of the Rorschach–Wikipedia debate. *Journal of Personality Assessment, 94,* 73–81.

Schumacher, E. F. (1973). Small is beautiful. *The Radical Humanist, 37*(5), 18–22.

Searls, D. (2017). *The inkblots: Hermann Rorschach, his iconic test, and the power of seeing.* New York, NY: Crown.

Sherman, M. (1952). A comparison of fermal and content factors in the diagnostic testing of schizophrenia. *Genetic Psychology Monographs, 46,* 184–234.

Shipley, W. C., Gruber, C. P., Martin, T. A., & Klein, A. M. (2009). *Shipley–2: Manual.* Los Angeles, CA: Western Psychological Services.

Siemsen, R. A. (1999). Relationships of Rorschach and MMPI–2 variables to the Hare Psychopathy Checklist—Revised among mentally ill incarcerated felons. *Dissertation Abstracts International: Section B. Sciences and Engineering, 60,* 2367.

Silberg, J. L., & Armstrong, J. G. (1992). The Rorschach test for predicting suicide among depressed adolescent inpatients. *Journal of Personality Assessment, 59,* 290–303. http://dx.doi.org/10.1207/s15327752jpa5902_6

Silva, D. (2002). The effect of color on productivity on Card X of the Rorschach. *Rorschachiana, 25,* 123–138. http://dx.doi.org/10.1027/1192-5604.25.1.123

Silverstein, M. L. (2007). *Disorders of the self: A personality-guided approach.* Washington, DC: American Psychological Association. http://dx.doi.org/10.1037/11490-000

Small, A., Teagno, L., Madero, J., Gross, H., & Ebert, M. (1982). A comparison of anorexics and schizophrenics on psychodiagnostic measures. *International Journal of Eating Disorders, 1,* 49–56. http://dx.doi.org/10.1002/1098-108X(198221)1:3<49::AID-EAT2260010306>3.0.CO;2-O

Smith, B. L. (1997). White bird: Flight from the terror of empty space. In J. R. Meloy, M. W. Acklin, C. B. Gacono, J. F. Murray, & C. A. Peterson (Eds.), *Contemporary Rorschach interpretation* (pp. 191–215). Mahwah, NJ: Erlbaum.

Smith, S. R., Bistis, K., Zahka, N. E., & Blais, M. A. (2007). Perceptual–organizational characteristics of the Rorschach task. *The Clinical Neuropsychologist, 21,* 789–799. http://dx.doi.org/10.1080/13854040600800995

Strickland, V. L. (2006). A descriptive study of boys with AD/HD referred for special education evaluation. *Dissertation Abstracts International: Section B. Sciences and Engineering, 67*(2), 170.

Thurber, J. (1942, November 14). The catbird seat. *The New Yorker,* pp. 17–20.

Tibon, S. (2000). Personality traits and peace negotiations: Integrative complexity and attitudes toward the Middle East peace process. *Group Decision and Negotiation, 9,* 1–15. http://dx.doi.org/10.1023/A:1008779305643

Tibon Czopp, S., & Zeligman, R. (2016). The Rorschach Comprehensive System (CS) psychometric validity of individual variables. *Journal of Personality Assessment, 98,* 335–342. http://dx.doi.org/10.1080/00223891.2015.1131162

Traenkle, K. A. (2002). An empirical evaluation of Rorschach white space scoring. *Dissertation Abstracts International: Section B. Sciences and Engineering, 62*(8), 3839.

Trenerry, M. R., & Pantle, M. L. (1990). MAPI code types in an inpatient crisis-unit sample. *Journal of Personality Assessment, 55,* 683–691. http://dx.doi.org/10.1080/00223891.1990.9674103

Urist, J. (1977). The Rorschach test and the assessment of object relations. *Journal of Personality Assessment, 41,* 3–9. http://dx.doi.org/10.1207/s15327752jpa4101_1

Vaillant, G. E. (1977). *Adaptation to life.* Boston, MA: Little, Brown.

van der Gaag, R. J., Caplan, R., van Engeland, H., Loman, F., & Buitelaar, J. K. (2005). A controlled study of formal thought disorder in children with autism and multiple complex developmental disorders. *Journal of Child and Adolescent Psychopharmacology, 15,* 465–476. http://dx.doi.org/10.1089/cap.2005.15.465

Vanem, P. C., Krog, D., & Hartmann, E. (2008). Assessment of substance abusers on the MCMI–III and the Rorschach. *Scandinavian Journal of Psychology, 49,* 83–91. http://dx.doi.org/10.1111/j.1467-9450.2007.00608.x

Viglione, D. J., Meyer, G. J., Resende, A. C., & Pignolo, C. (2017). A survey of challenges experienced by new learners coding the Rorschach. *Journal of Personality Assessment, 98,* 315–323.

Vijayakumaran, K. P., Ravindran, A., & Sahasranam, K. V. (1994). Rorschach indices of primary and secondary anxiety in the Exner Comprehensive System. *Journal of Psychological Researches, 38,* 14–18.

Vinson, D. B. (1960). Responses to the Rorschach test that identify thinking, feelings, and behavior. *Journal of Clinical & Experimental Psychopathology, 21,* 34–40.

Walters, R. H. (1953). A preliminary analysis of the Rorschach records of fifty prison inmates. *Journal of Projective Techniques, 17,* 437–446. http://dx.doi.org/10.1080/08853126.1953.10380509

Weber, C. A., Meloy, J. R., & Gacono, C. B. (1992). A Rorschach study of attachment and anxiety in inpatient conduct-disordered and dysthymic adolescents. *Journal of Personality Assessment, 58,* 16–26. http://dx.doi.org/10.1207/s15327752jpa5801_2

Weiner, I. B. (1994). The Rorschach Inkblot Method (RIM) is not a test: Implications for theory and practice. *Journal of Personality Assessment, 62,* 498–504. http://dx.doi.org/10.1207/s15327752jpa6203_9

Wood, J. M., Krishnamurthy, R., & Archer, R. P. (2003). Three factors of the Comprehensive System for the Rorschach and their relationship to Wechsler IQ scores in an adolescent sample. *Assessment, 10,* 259–265. http://dx.doi.org/10.1177/1073191103255493

Wood, J. M., Nezworski, M. T., Lilienfeld, S. O., & Garb, H. N. (2003). *What's wrong with the Rorschach?* San Francisco, CA: Jossey-Bass.

Wright, C. V., Beattie, S. G., Galper, D. I., Church, A. S., Bufka, L. F., Brabender, V. M., & Smith, B. L. (2017). Assessment practices of professional psychologists: Results of a national survey. *Professional Psychology: Research and Practice, 48,* 73–78. http://dx.doi.org/10.1037/pro0000086

Yalof, J. (2006). Case illustration of a boy with nonverbal learning disorder and Asperger's features: Neuropsychological and personality assessment. *Journal of Personality Assessment, 87,* 15–34. http://dx.doi.org/10.1207/s15327752jpa8701_02

Young, M. H., Justice, J., & Erdberg, P. (1999). Risk factors for violent behavior among incarcerated male psychiatric patients: A multimethod approach. *Assessment, 6,* 243–258. http://dx.doi.org/10.1177/107319119900600305

Zhong, S., Jing, J., Wang, L., & Yin, Q. (2007). Analysis on Rorschach Inkblot Test in children with attention deficit hyperactivity disorder. *Chinese Journal of Clinical Psychology, 15,* 545–547.

Zulliger, H., & Salomon, F. (1970). *El Test de Zulliger, un test individual y colectivo* [The Zulliger test, a collective and individual test]. Buenos Aires, Argentina: Editorial Kapelusz.

Index

About the Authors

James P. Choca, PhD, is a Cuban American with a doctorate in clinical psychology from Loyola University Chicago. He was a member of the faculty of the Psychology Division of the Northwestern University Medical School, and chief of psychology at Lakeside VA Medical Center for over 20 years. After moving to Roosevelt University, he first directed the clinical PsyD program and then served as chair of the department for 12 years. He is a full professor teaching courses in psychopathology and psychological assessment. A diplomate of the American Board of Assessment Psychology, and a fellow of the Society for Personality Assessment, Dr. Choca's scholarly work has included writings on the Millon Clinical Multiaxial Inventory and the Halstead Category Test. More recently he created the Emotional Assessment System (EAS-5), a measure of disorders in the fifth edition of the *Diagnostic and Statistical Manual of Mental Disorders*. His interest in the evaluations of Hispanics recently led to his working in Chile, Argentina, and Spain.

Edward D. Rossini, PhD, is a professor of psychology at Roosevelt University in Chicago, Illinois. He has a long-standing interest in lifespan personality assessment and has presented and published on the Rorschach and the Thematic Apperception Test. He graduated from the clinical psychology program at Loyola University Chicago, which was a Klopfer-based Rorschach program directed by "our Herr Rorschach," the late Dr. Frank J. Kobler.